Make Your Mark:
A Handbook for Learning
Free-Motion Quilting

KIMBERLY DAVIS

ISBN: 150324542X
ISBN-13: 9781503245426

DEDICATION

For Kevin,
With Deepest Love
For Everything

ACKNOWLEDGMENTS

At times our own light goes out and is rekindled by a spark from another person.
Each of us has cause to think with deep gratitude of those who have lighted the flame within us.

~ Albert Schweitzer

Thanks to my mother, Cheryl Schofield, who always supported my obsessions, no matter where they led. I couldn't have asked for a more loving environment to follow my passions.
And to my grandmother, Delores Haarala, for always cheering me on.
And to my brother, Mark Schofield, who keeps me laughing.

Cynthia Spencer is an amazing business partner and even more amazing friend, who has been encouraging me to write, create, and otherwise get my work out in to the world for almost as long as I have known her.

Thanks to Bobbie Muscarella, for being my first quilting teacher and starting me on this amazing journey.

Connie Hozvicka helped me deepen my creative practice and taught me so much about what it means to live a heart-centered and creative life.

Kate Robertson coached me through the early stages and reminded me to take small steps. Hali Karla was there throughout—keeping me accountable and providing wise and loving support. And the Dreamholders (Michelle Turbide, Cynthia Lee, Betsy Cañas Garmon, and Jes Gordon) so wonderfully held space for my dreams.

Meredith Weber did a fabulous line edit. (It goes without saying that any typos are mine and mine alone!) Tina Hay helped with photo editing.

And thanks to the hundreds of students from whom I've learned so much with over the past decade. Your willingness to learn and be beginners has been inspirational.

Table of Contents

FINDING YOUR VOICE

QUILTING FOR REAL

A VERY SPECIAL LETTER ABOUT LEARNING

To My Dear Free-Motion Quilting Friend,

Congratulations! Do you know just how much you rock? You do. Very much!

How do I know this? Because you bought this handbook. That proves how awesome you are. You have great taste in writers (you do!) and even more importantly you are taking the first step towards learning a new skill or improving an existing one.

And that just rocks!

And so I want to welcome you to this handbook and invite you to cozy up with it for a bit. This handbook may be a little different from other free-motion quilt (FMQ) books because of the learning philosophy I've developed after introducing hundreds of people to FMQ for more than a decade.

As adults, we forget what it means to be a beginner. That's not to say that we lose the ability to learn, but we often lose our ability to be comfortable with the beginning stages of learning. We are used to being good at things and don't often encounter situations where we need to learn something completely new. So in my classes, we practice the skills required for FMQ **and** we talk about the process of learning new creative skills. To me, they go hand in hand. When we understand the *process* of learning it makes the *practice* of learning go more smoothly.

I call this a handbook because that is what it is. It is a book for working—for doing. I know how easy it is to collect books, thinking that somehow the knowledge will transfer to us through osmosis. (I really must think that—it would explain the large stack of books that rests upon my nightstand.) But that rarely works, at least in my experience.

Learning free-motion quilting is like learning any new skill: it takes intentional practice. The only way to learn a skill is by doing it.

Benjamin Franklin put it best:

> *Tell me and I forget.*
>
> *Teach me and I remember.*
>
> *Involve me and I learn.*

My intention is to create a handbook that will *involve* you.

I'll guide you through a series of practice exercises that build upon each other. If you were taking this class with me, I could provide you with immediate feedback for each exercise and let you know what you were doing well, what you needed to improve, and most importantly, how you can improve. But alas, I cannot be everywhere. What I can do, however, is help you learn to evaluate your own work.

With each exercise, I provide instructions not only on how to quilt the patterns, but also guidance on how to evaluate and assess your progress. Learning takes place not just through the doing, but in the evaluation of what has been done. Don't let the evaluation process scare you off: the point is to learn what you are doing well and where you can improve. It's not about inviting your inner critic to join in (but more on that later).

My hope is that once you have worked through this book then you can learn any quilting pattern on your own by breaking the pattern into smaller parts and then evaluating your lines, shapes, and stitches

In addition to the exercises presented, much of skill learning takes place in the mind—in understanding what is going on when we learn something new. And so I've included a series of short notes that explain different parts of the learning process. These are the messages about learning that I share in my in-person classes and they often spark interesting discussions. I'll also provide questions and prompts for you to reflect on your own experiences in the learning process.

Learning anything new is a journey and I am honored to be your guide.

Warmly,

Kimberly Davis

Learning Free-Motion Quilting

Let's begin by talking about the special challenges of learning free-motion quilting. One of the main things I emphasize in my classes is that learning how to free-motion quilt takes practice, but you need to practice smart. That is, you need to understand what you will be learning and break it down into smaller steps.

One challenge is that you are trying to learn two new skills at once

- ❑ First, you are learning how to coordinate the foot pedal speed (how fast the needle moves up and down) and your hand movements (how fast you move the quilt under the needle) to create consistently even stitches. This is the technical side of FMQ. For some, this is like trying to pat your head and rub your tummy at the same time.

- ❑ Second, you are learning how to make art decisions—where to place your stitches, how many and what kind of stitches to create, and where to go next while stitching out a particular design. This is the creative side. I call it making *art decisions*, but it doesn't mean you have to be an artist.

This is similar to the things we needed to master when learning to drive a car. You started learning to drive in parking lots and quiet back roads before venturing onto busier roads and then eventually onto the highway. You had to learn the mechanics of controlling the car before you could begin to navigate through traffic. The same holds true for learning free-motion quilting: **you need to learn the mechanics of creating consistent stitches and smooth curves before venturing out to make the art decisions involved in stitching motifs.**

I've written this handbook to help you simplify your learning process. You'll practice one skill at a time, and each exercise will build on the ones that came before.

- ❑ First, you'll focus on **creating consistent stitches** by experimenting with how your foot pedal speed and hand-movement speed interact. This is like learning to drive a car: knowing how much pressure to put on the gas pedal and how quickly or sharply to turn the steering wheel. Similarly, with free-motion quilting you need to learn how much pressure to put on the foot pedal to control needle speed and how fast to move the quilt.

- ❑ Once you feel comfortable creating even stitches, you will begin learning to **control the placement of your stitches**. Like learning to drive a car, this is moving from driving in an empty parking lot, where you can focus strictly on the mechanics of the gas and brake pedals, to driving down quiet roads where you need to stay in your lane. In FMQ, some of the skills you'll be learning include estimating the sizes of stitches, gauging the distances between motifs, and creating curves that are smooth and points that are sharp.

- ❑ Then you'll practice making **art decisions** and stitching different motifs. During driver's ed, this would be like navigating around the commercial part of town or merging onto and off of a busy highway. Here, you'll concentrate on filling space and beginning to create your own designs. You'll also consider what types of designs and motifs feel natural and reflect your personal style.

❑ Throughout the learning process I will offer you ways to **assess your stitches and quilting lines**. One part of learning a skill is being able to provide yourself with feedback. This means looking at your stitches and figuring out what is going well and what can be improved. Be gentle with yourself as you evaluate your learning. Imagine yourself offering feedback to a child or loved one learning a new skill. Think about how encouraging you would be and how positively you would frame discussions about improvement. Direct that gentle loving energy towards yourself.

❑ You will also discover **Learning Notes** throughout the text. These are the insights and ideas that I share with my in-person students. These notes can help you understand how you are learning and how you can use your natural learning process to learn more effectively. These notes will explore learning and expression, and help you discover the beauty in the unique and creative marks that you quilt.

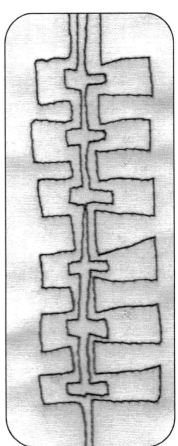

Choosing Supplies

When embarking on a journey, you need to pack the right supplies. Just as a GPS with outdated maps can lead you astray when traveling, using the wrong products while learning can make it harder to learn. Let the following be your packing guide.

- ❑ **Sewing machine**. You don't need a fancy machine. As long as you have a darning foot and can drop or cover your feed dogs, then you can free-motion quilt. Just make sure that your machine is clean and in good working order—this will make life easier.

  If your sewing machine cannot drop the feed dogs and doesn't come with a cover, you can improvise one with an index card. Use a hole punch to create a hole in the center of the card and then cover the feed dogs with it, making sure to align the punched hole with the needle hole. Keep it in place with painter's tape.

  I've taught people to free-motion quilt on top-of-the-line computerized sewing machines and on the most basic mechanical machines that have been passed down through the family. It's not the age or cost of the machine that matters, but the quality of the stitch. Some vintage machines have gorgeous stitches and some newer machines stitch poorly right out of the box.

  That said there are two features to consider when shopping for a new or new-to-you sewing machine: a **needle-down function** and the **size of the throat space**. You also may want to consider investing in a **custom table or cabinet** for your machine.

  A **needle-down function** is really helpful for machine quilting. Let's say you stop quilting to answer the phone. When you stop stitching with a regular sewing machine (one without a needle-down function), the machine stops whenever you stop. Sometimes it stops with the needle above the quilt and the darning foot not fully pressed on the quilt. So as you get up to answer the phone, the quilt slips, the thread pulls, and you are left having to deal with a really large stitch.

  If you want to keep your existing machine without a needle-down setting, develop the habit of making sure that the needle is down when you stop stitching. Every time you stop stitching, turn the flywheel toward you until the needle lowers into the quilt. Then you can answer the phone without worrying about the quilt.

  If you want to buy a new machine, look for one that has a needle-down function, in which the machine always stops with the darning foot firmly engaged on the quilt and the needle down.

  The other thing to consider when shopping for a new machine is the **size of the throat space**; that is the space between the body of the sewing machine (on the right) and the head of the machine (on the left). Larger throat spaces make it easier to maneuver the bulk of larger quilts.

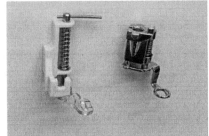

- **Darning foot**. A darning foot has an offset shank and a spring. Some have a small bar that goes over the needle screw and helps the foot hop as you stitch. It's the hopping that allows you to glide the quilt under the presser foot.

- **Thread**. Begin with good quality, 50-weight 100% cotton thread that contrasts with the fabric you plan to use for your practice and learning. As you improve your skills, you can use some of the glorious metallic, rayon or polyester threads. But these can break easily, so make it easier on yourself and begin with cotton.

- **80/12 Jeans Needle**. These needles have sharper points, so they pierce the fabric cleanly, creating smoother stitches. They are also more durable. That said, please change your needles often—after every 6-8 hours of stitching. Really.

- **18" square quilt sandwiches made from 100% cotton fabric or muslin and with 100% cotton batting sandwiched between**. You will need many sandwiches to work through this entire handbook, but begin with at least six. This allows you to learn without worrying about running out.

  Although it is tempting to use up our old fabrics (like poly-cotton blends) and high-loft, polyester battings, they tend to not behave as well or look as good as cotton batting does when quilted. Invest in your skill building by using quality materials for learning.

- **Sewing machine cabinet or extension table (optional)**. It's much easier to slide the quilt around on a larger surface. A custom sewing machine table or cabinet helps with machine quilting by providing a larger surface for the quilt to glide on as you stitch. You can buy an oversized Plexiglas extension table custom-made for your machine that rests on top of your working table. Or you can purchase cabinets with a hole in the table top so your machine rests on a lower shelf and the quilt lays flush on the working surface.

- A couple tools that are very helpful, but optional, are a **Teflon-coated sheet** for the machine bed and **machine quilting gloves**. You can purchase both at local quilt shops. Having a Teflon surface helps the quilt slide around the table more easily. The ones for quilting come with a sticky back and a hole for the needle. Machine quilting gloves help you to control the quilt sandwich as you quilt.

- **Sketchbook and pencil**. Believe it or not, a lot of learning free-motion quilting actually happens on paper. I keep a sketchbook by my sewing machine and practice patterns on paper before I ever try to stitch them. This doesn't need to be a fancy thing—even computer paper printed on one side and rescued from the recycle bin works. I do like a bound book because it lets me flip through for ideas, but you can always keep loose sheets in a binder or a folder.

- **An open mind and a compassionate heart**. Allow yourself to be a beginner and treat yourself gently. Many of the **Learning Notes** that follow will further explore navigating the challenges of learning in a gentle and kind way.

On Paper Practice & Quilt Practice

Throughout this handbook I'll suggest that you work on paper first and practice drawing the design again and again. This mindful practice is how I approach quilting.

My constant companion when I am machine quilting is my sketchbook and pencil. This practice sketchbook sits next to my sewing machine and is the place where I try out new quilt designs. I use a pencil because having a pen or marker near a quilt can be bad news. I have been known to accidently mark my quilt top with an open marker that rested on my sewing table. It's much easier to remove accidental marks made by pencil then by a pen or marker.

I only try to stitch a design once I've practice drawing it again and again. I usually wait until I start to feel a little bored with drawing—that sense of "enough already, let's get to stitching." At that point, I know that I have become comfortable with the art decisions involved in creating the design. Sketchbook practice helps ingrain the pattern in my mind and in my muscles so that I don't have to think about the design as much when I am stitching. That allows me to quilt with ease and confidence, which makes my marks look effortless.

Although you can use loose paper for practice, I think having a bound sketchbook is valuable. I can flip through it for inspiration. What ideas have I played with in the past? Maybe seeing the juxtaposition of two designs inspires a third. Sometimes I see old patterns in new ways and that sets me down a new road of quilting designs.

I also keep a practice quilt sandwich nearby. Once I feel comfortable drawing, I will take a test drive and try the pattern on my practice sandwich before approaching my quilt top. This is especially important for more complicated designs.

The more you practice, the more comfortable you will feel and that comfortable confidence will translate to your quilting.

To me it's not so much that practice makes perfect as it is that practice makes comfort. And when we feel comfortable then we can be more expressive with our marks.

The Hand of the Artist and FMQ

I've included many different types of FMQ samples throughout this book. These represent my particular style, which is a result of the way I see the world and the types of marks that I make naturally with my hands. Some samples are quilted and some are drawn. I've included both types for interest and to begin to give you a sense of how drawn designs appear when stitched. To illustrate the learning notes, I've also included different designs to show how you can combine motifs to create new designs. These are shown rounded rectangles and are for your inspiration and as a starting point for your own designs.

Don't strive to make your work look like mine. Use them as inspiration only and let your own eyes, hands, and heart take you in your own direction. The work of your hands will be entirely yours. Celebrate it! It's a gift to world to be able to share your unique vision.

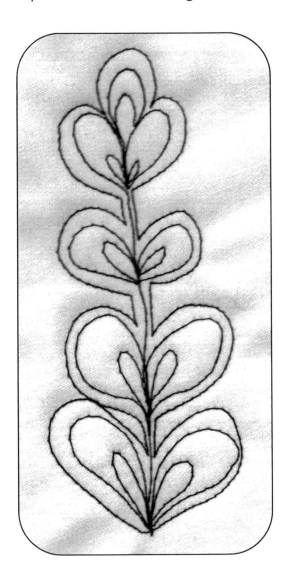

Exercise: Sewing Machine Setup

Objective: To learn how to setup your sewing machine for free-motion quilting

❑ **Make sure your sewing machine** is in good working order before your begin. Find your sewing machine's instruction book and clean your machine. If you haven't cleaned it in a while, you may be amazed at the quantities of dust and lint that have collected. Your machine will purr after its cleaning. If it's been a while since you've had it serviced, you may wish to take it to a repair shop. Regular service can help maintain the longevity of your machine.

Check your manual and see if your machine needs to be oiled regularly. Some machines do and others do not. If in doubt, ask your sewing machine dealer.

❑ **Thread your machine with 100% cotton, 50-weight thread.**

❑ **Wind several bobbins with the same thread** so that you can practice a lot without having to stop to reload bobbins.

❑ **Choose a thread color that contrasts with your quilt sandwiches.** This will allow you to see and evaluate your stitches and quilting designs.

❑ Insert a new **Sharp or Jeans/Denim 80/12 needle.** Change your needles after every 6 or so hours of quilting. Really.

❑ Change to a **darning foot.** If you don't have one, contact your sewing machine dealer. **Drop or cover your feed dogs.** The combination of darning foot and dropped or covered feed dogs is what enables you to work free-motion.

❑ If you have an **extension table or a cabinet** for your machine, use it. It's much easier to slide the quilt around on a larger surface.

❑ If your machine has a **needle-down feature, engage it.** If you don't have needle down, then get into the habit of making sure the needle is down whenever you stop stitching.

❑ If you **normally sew in your socks or slippers,** then do so! Make yourself as comfortable as you can so you can really settle into the learning process.

❑ If you don't have a sewing machine cabinet, it can be more comfortable to **sit on a cushion or pillow** so that you are more level with the sewing machine bed. Try it and see how it feels.

Exercise: Preparing Quilt Sandwiches for Practicing

Objectives

o   To learn how to prepare the three layers (backing, batting, and top) for quilting

o   To learn the difference between spray basting, fusible basting, and pin basting

For your first practice exercises, you will be working on a small scale, and the quilt sandwiches will be easy to maneuver. I recommend that you make at least six practice sandwiches to start.

For each sandwich you make, you need two 18" squares of muslin or other plain and light-colored 100% cotton fabric. You also need an 18" square of 100% cotton, mid-loft batting. For these exercises, you can baste the three layers together using safety pins, a fusible spray, or fusible batting or web.

Effective basting can make your quilting easier and keep puckers and bubbles from developing. I use different basting techniques for different size quilts. For quilts that are crib-size or smaller, I prefer spray basting with 505 spray adhesive. For larger quilts, I pin baste. I've also been exploring using a lightweight fusible web, like Heat-n-Bond Featherlight, for the most secure hold. This will, of course, add stiffness to your quilt, which can be good for a wallhanging, but not so good for a crib quilt.

Spray Basting: Lay your backing right side down on the table or floor. You may want to cover the surrounding surfaces with newspaper or a plastic sheet to protect them from the spray adhesive. Lightly spray the backing. Carefully smooth the batting on the backing. Lightly spray the batting. Carefully place the quilt top on the batting. Smooth all three layers.

Fusible Batting or Web: If you are using fusible batting, follow the packaging instructions. If you want to use a fusible web, choose one that is lightweight and sewable. Read the instructions and fuse the web to the wrong sides of the backing and the quilt top. Lay the batting on the table and make sure it is smooth. Remove the paper from the fused backing fabric, if applicable, and place the backing fusible side down on the batting. Smooth. Beginning in the center, fuse the backing to the batting, being careful not to fuse wrinkles or pleats. After the backing is fused, flip the partial sandwich and lay the quilt top on the batting. Repeat to fuse the web in place.

Pin Basting: Lay your backing right side down on the table or floor. If basting on a table, try to raise it higher to save your back. Tape or clip the backing to your table or floor to keep it smooth, but don't pull it taut. If your backing is too tight, it will cause puckers.

Carefully lay the batting and then the quilt top on the backing. Smooth all three layers. Begin basting with pins and work from the center out. Smaller safety pins (size 1 or 2) leave smaller holes in your quilt.

You've basted enough when you can place your hand anywhere on the quilt and feel a pin. You can remove the safety pins as you quilt.

While safety pins are a secure basting method, they can make quilting difficult. They can get caught on the edge of your sewing machine table, which can cause resistance and pull the quilt. And also, lots of pins make your quilt heavier to maneuver. For these practice sandwiches, these issues won't cause lots of problems, but when quilting a larger quilt you may want to be aware of them.

My strategy for pin-basted, larger quilts is to start by quilting in the ditch (which is to quilt machine-guided straight lines using a walking foot; generally along the seam allowances). Then remove as many pins as I can before I start free-motion quilting. The ditch stitching stabilizes the layers so they won't shift while you free-motion quilt. And the ability to remove safety pins before free-motion quilting helps to lighten your load.

If you want to ditch stitch before free-motion quilting, then watch pin placement as you are basting, and avoid placing pins across or near seams.

Practice Quilt Sandwich Liberation

To do anything very well you have to 'allow' (not to force, not to make) yourself do it, and the way to do that is to do it over and over again, so that you teach your body how to do it and it becomes second nature - you don't have to think about it anymore.

~Ron Monsma

When I teach in-person, I encourage my students to make sure that their muslin quilt sandwiches look terrible before they leave class. "That's how you'll know you were really practicing and learning," I'll tell them.

And so I offer you the same freedom. As you work through the exercises, make sure to cover the sandwiches with quilting. Stitch with abandon and give yourself the freedom to make an unsightly mess. When you allow yourself the freedom to play, learning happens in very surprising ways. Often by playing, we create new combinations of shapes and lines, discovering new ideas for quilting designs.

After you have covered your sandwich with quilting, you may want to write the date on it. Keep your early practice sandwiches so that you can see your improvement. I didn't and I have always regretted it—both as a way to see the improvement as I learned to free-motion quilt and to share with my students that I did indeed begin as you are.

Exercise: Learn to Begin and End a Line of Free-Motion Quilting

Objectives

- Learn how to secure stitches at the beginning and end of lines of quilting.

- Learn how to secure stitches when a thread breaks or runs out in the middle of a line of quilting.

Bring Bobbin Thread to Top of the Quilt Sandwich

Whenever you start free-motion quilting, you need to make sure that you bring your bobbin thread to the top of the quilt. By doing so, you avoid the jams that result when the bobbin thread get pulled down by the feed dogs, and you avoid stitching over the bobbin thread, which makes an unsightly mess on the back that is hard to remove.

1. To bring the bobbin thread to the top, place the quilt sandwich under your presser foot where you would like to begin quilting. Lower the presser foot.

2. Now take one stitch by hand, turning the flywheel towards you. Make sure that you complete the stitch by raising the needle to its highest position. Notice that the darning foot slightly raises from the surface of the quilt as well.

3. Tug on the top thread, and the bobbin thread will rise to the top of your quilt sandwich.

4. Hold both top and bottom threads out of the way and drop the presser foot.

Beginning and Ending a Line of Free-Motion Quilting with Securing Stitches

When you begin or end a line of free-motion quilting, you need to secure the threads so your stitches don't come undone. The easiest way to fasten your stitches is to take 4-5 tiny stitches while barely moving. These tiny stitches are secure and difficult to remove. Don't just stitch in one spot—this forms a knot on the back of the quilt. Instead, barely move your hands.

Once you have taken these securing stitches, begin quilting. Cut the thread tails after you've moved an inch or so away from the starting location. If you cut too soon, you might accidentally cut through the thread in the needle, which means that you need to start over.

Burying Thread Tails

An option that some people prefer is to leave their thread tails and bury them in the batting of the quilt after stitching. This helps to blend your beginning and ending completely with the rest of the quilting. In this case, do not take the securing stitches at the beginning and end of the quilting line, but leave the thread tails hanging. At the end of your quilting, you thread the tails on a needle and bury the stitches.

When the Thread Breaks or Runs Out

Sometimes thread runs out or breaks in the middle of a line of stitching. When that happens you need to stop, rethread the machine and/or rewind a bobbin. Then take a small pair of scissors and trim the top thread and bobbin thread tails even with the quilt top. Now, position that needle so that it is located 1" prior to the thread break. Pull the bobbin thread to the top and take a few small stitches to secure the ends. Now carefully stitch over approximately 1" of stitching before the thread broke. This will secure those ends in place. Continue quilting your design.

Here you can see that I ran out of bobbin thread on the right. Trim the right thread tail.

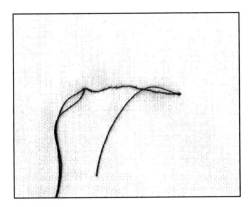

Now, as explained above, bring up the bobbin about 1" before the end of stitching. In the picture below, these are the second set of threads to the right. Overlap the initial stitching line using tiny stitches: and then continue on your way. The dotted brackets show the overlapped area.

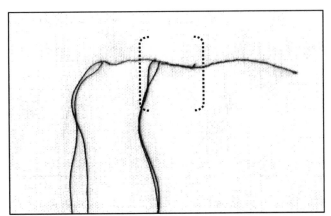

Exercise: Coordinating Foot Pedal and Hand Movement Speeds

Objectives

o Learn how foot pedal and hand movement speeds interact to create stitches of different lengths.

o Coordinate foot pedal and hand movement speeds to create consistent stitches.

o Find combinations of foot pedal and hand movement speeds that feel comfortable and create consistent stitches.

So you've set up your sewing machine, made a few practice sandwiches, and learned to start and end a line of quilting. Now it's time to begin coordinating your foot and hand movements.

Sit at your sewing machine. Make sure that you are seated at a comfortable height. Place the quilt sandwich under the needle where you would like to begin quilting. Bring the bobbin thread to the top and secure your stitches.

Now it's time to play with quilting. I call it playing because you aren't going to try to quilt anything in particular. Instead, you are going to practice smart and focus on coordinating your needle speed (determined by the pressure you put on the foot pedal) and how fast you move the quilt under the needle (determined by the speed of your hand movement).

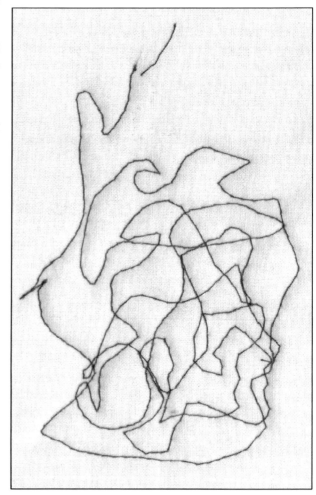

First, you will learn **how foot pedal speed and your hand movement interact**. Begin by quilting random, unplanned lines—moving the quilt top forward and backwards, diagonally, and side to side under the needle. You aren't trying to go anywhere or create anything in particular.

Notice that you don't need to pivot the quilt to sew around a curve or to change direction. It is easier to machine quilt a full-size quilt using free-motion rather than straight lines because you don't have to rotate or turn the quilt under the sewing machine throat.

What you stitch should look like a random mess of overlapping lines. Don't worry, it should look ugly!

Experiment with different combinations of hand movement speeds and foot pedal speeds. What combination feels comfortable for you?

o   Try putting less pressure on the foot pedal (needle moves slower) and moving your hands faster—notice that your stitch length increases.

o   With a faster foot pedal (needle moves faster) and slower hands, your stitches become much smaller.

o   If your machine has a motor control, try setting it to 75% or 50%. Note that it slows down the stitching speed, so slow your hand movements accordingly.

Do you feel like you have more control now?

Fast needle and slow hands make little stitches and smoother lines...

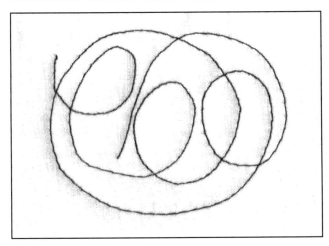

Slower needle and slower hands make bigger stitches and more jagged lines...

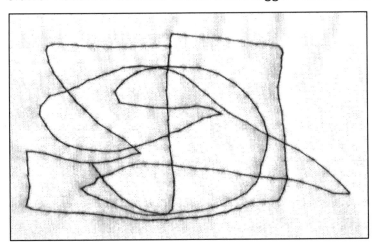

When you are beginning to feel comfortable with this movement, try random curves, swoops, and scribbles. Don't try to stipple or plan where you are quilting—you're just trying to get used to coordinating your foot pedal speed and hand movement.

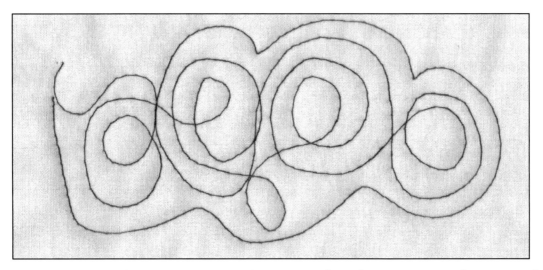

Keep playing until you are creating the size stitches that you want; that is, stitches that are consistent and neither too big nor too small. Your goal is to find that sweet spot where your hands and feet feel comfortable.

Look at this again: Larger stitches create rougher curves (left) than smaller stitches (right).

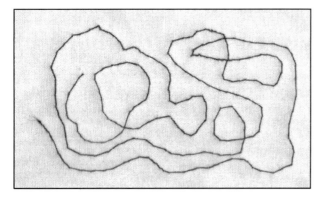 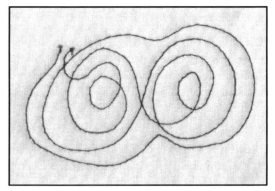

Stitches that are too small are difficult to remove should you want or need to rip them out. Over time, you will find creating your desired stitch length becomes second nature.

Check Your Hand Position

Take a moment and check out how you are holding your hands on the quilt. Proper hand position can have a big impact on how your quilting looks and how your body feels. It is common for beginners to grab the quilt to maneuver it under the needle. Grabbing seems like it should offer you the most control, but that is deceptive.

Take a look at the quilt under the needle. Notice how it is wrinkled and puffy. There is a lot of wiggle room, which makes it harder to control the quilt.

Also, notice how your shoulders tense up when you grab the quilt this way. A long session quilting like this can do a number on your body.

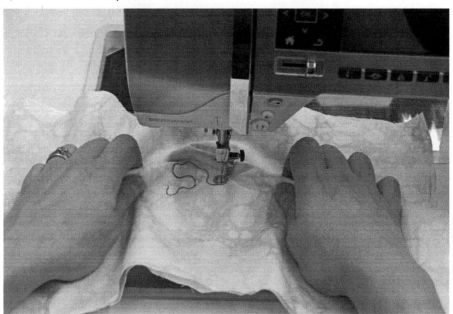

The ideal hand position is shown below. Hold them flat, and frame the needle with your thumbs and fingers. This provides more contact with the quilt and with the sewing machine bed or table.

This position also helps keep your shoulders down, which is easier on the body.

Two things make maneuvering the quilt this way easier when you are first learning. One is a pair of machine quilting gloves with finger grips that help you control the quilt. The other is a Teflon sheet on the bed or table.

If you have an extension table or sewing machine cabinet, it provides a larger surface area for stitching.

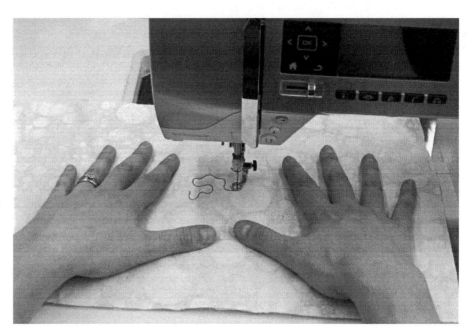

Gentle Evaluations

o When you need to shift your hand positions on the quilt sandwich because you are running out of room, be careful not to lift both hands while still running the machine Beginners often keep running the foot pedal when shifting their hands on the quilt sandwich. I've even watched new quilters lift their hands to their face to adjust their glasses while still pressing on the foot pedal. This can cause unwanted jigs and jags in the quilting line.

o If you need to adjust your hands or your glasses, stop quilting by stopping your hands and your feet, make the necessary adjustment, and then start back up. Over time, you will learn to be able to adjust one hand at a time, while slowing down your foot pedal speed.

o Keep practicing, paying attention to the foot pedal and hand movement speeds that feel comfortable.

o Your muslin sandwich should be covered with lines crossing and turning. Don't worry about what it looks like overall, just focus on how the stitches look. Are you becoming more consistent? Good. Once you start to feel comfortable, then you can move onto the next exercise.

Next Steps

The next few sections provide a little bit of reassurance about some innate abilities that we may not even know that we have.

- We are **natural pattern finders**.

- We each have a unique set of **consistent inconsistencies.**

These two abilities work together and help us learn to quilt as we begin to estimate distances and sizes of motifs and evaluate our work. I'll talk about them both over the next few pages.

But even with all our amazing abilities, we are sometimes visited by an unwelcome guest—our inner critics. We'll also talk about learning to identify the negative messages from our inner critics and how to flip them around.

Humans as Pattern Finders

Humans are natural pattern finders. We look for patterns all the time. Think about gazing at clouds on a warm summer day. You might find a clown face, a castle, or a cow floating in the wisps of white.

This works to our advantage when free-motion quilting—we just have to trust in it. If we are quilting a large space, perhaps a border, with a repeating motif, like the pebbly circles below, we may look at our first circle and think "That's a bit misshapen." And then we stitch the second motif and think "That's more like a fat oval than a circle." At this point, we might get discouraged and rip out what we've done. Or we might just stop, shove the quilt into a grocery bag, and leave it to age.

But here's the beautiful thing about pattern finding—the more times that something is repeated the less the individual variation matters. Instead, the mind looks and says "Hey! Cool pebbles!" So trust and keep on keeping on. Don't stop.

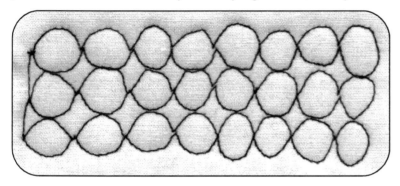

You'll see this as you examine the samples in this book. Each motif is a little different and has its own personality. At the same time, there are similarities that make them feel related. And that makes our pattern-finding brain very happy.

Our Consistent Inconsistencies

We all have unique handwriting. It's easy to become familiar with the different writing styles of family, friends, and co-workers. Think about receiving a handwritten envelope in the mail. You often know who it is from just seeing the address. But if you were to stop and study the details of their writing, you would probably notice that each letter looks a little different. Nobody's handwriting is exactly the same from letter to letter, word to word, or even sentence to sentence. Because the inconsistencies fall within a similar range their personal handwriting style comes through.

Copy the following sentence five times—each on its own line. Be fluid and loose as you write.

I am happy to practice free-motion quilting and allow myself the freedom to learn.

_____

_____

_____

_____

_____

Compare the five lines of text. They may look similar because they were written by the same hand, but they are not exactly the same. This illustrates the tolerances of your handwriting, or what I call your _consistent inconsistencies_.

Your handwriting looks like your own and nobody else's. It flows from your pen comfortably and naturally. You don't have to think about it because it is a natural part of your self-expression. If you've ever tried to copy someone else's handwriting, you know how awkward that can feel. You need to think about every letter and the connection between them. And yet when you return to your own handwriting, it feels comfortable again.

The same holds for our free-motion quilting. When I teach beginners, it becomes pretty clear early on that each student has their own style of quilting. At the end of class, each quilted practice sandwich clearly belongs to a particular student.

So to return to the example of quilting pebbly circles, as you are humming along, stitching the side border, you are bringing your personal style to the quilt. What your inner critic may see as wobbles actually represent your consistent inconsistencies and quite literally show your hand as the maker.

So celebrate your wobbles and blips, especially as you are learning. They are distinctly yours and yours alone. No one else will wobble exactly like you. And that's a beautiful thing.

Did you notice that I slipped a positive affirmation into the sentence you repeated above? Being a beginner is a lot easier when we allow ourselves the freedom to learn. Part of our giving ourselves the freedom to learn is watching our self-talk. If you find yourself slipping into negative self-talk, amend it with a positive twist as soon as you notice it. So, "Boy, this is so hard, I don't think I will ever learn how," can be changed to "Boy, this is so hard, but if I keep practicing and give myself the freedom to learn, I know that I will improve."

This brings us to a subject that comes up frequently when I'm teaching free-motion quilting. How do we respond to our inner critics?

Dealing with Your Inner Critic

Before we begin with the FMQ exercises, let's take a moment to talk about inner critics. When I teach, I listen carefully to my students' self-talk and descriptions of their work and process for the negative messages that tell me that their inner critic has been activated. That spurs a discussion about observing our self-talk, watching for negative messages, and learning how to transform a negative message into a more positive, liberating one. Since I cannot be with you as you learn, I want you to keep watch for the negative self-talk that comes from your inner critic.

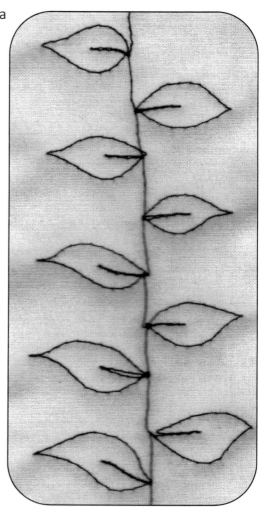

Inner critics are one of the most common obstacles to learning something new. They don't allow us to be a beginner. They hold us to such high standards that we can't go through the fumbling stages of learning. If you don't have an inner critic, consider yourself blessed! But for the rest of us, inner gremlins are completely normal, if annoying and troublesome. When we begin something new it is very common to hear little voices of doubt and criticism. "You'll never be able to do this." "That looks terrible, why don't you give up?" "Why are you wasting this fabric and time?"

Sometimes we're not aware that we are hearing those messages. We sit down to practice our free-motion quilting and then have an irresistible urge to put away laundry or alphabetize our spices. That's resistance and that comes from the inner critic too.

Inner critics try to sabotage your efforts, convince you that you are a failure, and encourage you to spend the rest of your days on the couch watching Real Housewives. Why would they do that?

As with most things that are worth it, the process of creation is rewarding and challenging in turn. While I believe that creation is the natural state of our inner being, it can also be laden with obstacles that stop us in our tracks. You've probably experienced these blocks in many different ways. Maybe you wanted to a new project, but you were immediately fraught with doubts about your ability. Maybe you hear a chorus of negative messages when you sit down to create: "It's not good enough." "It's ugly." "Who do you think you're fooling?" Or maybe your desire to create is countered by a deep resistance—instead of heading to your sewing machine, you find yourself scrubbing grout, playing around on Facebook, or sorting socks.

If our natural state of being is creation, where do these blocks come from? The honest answer is that they come from our inner critics. Our inner critics (or gremlins—I like to call mine a gremlin because it makes him sound more cartoony and less scary) are a mash-up of memories from childhood, messages from society, anxieties and fears, judgments, negative feelings, and lots of other icky things that we have accreted onto our creative being over the years. These negative messages cling to us and hide our light.

I believe that our inner critics are trying to keep us safe, but use very perverse (and sometimes very effective) methods to do so. Our inner critics want us to stay in our comfort zone. They want us to stay with what we know. And this can be okay. But if you are reading this book, then you are most likely looking to break out of your box, escape your comfort zone, and approach the unknown. This means that at some point you will be faced with confronting your inner critic.

What makes our inner critics so powerful is that they use lies, misdirection, and irrelevancies to stop us in our tracks. They tell us things that we wouldn't dream of saying to someone we love—or even to someone we dislike. And yet we listen and even buy into what they say.

The first step in countering our inner critics is to be able to identify when they are speaking. We have an almost constant internal monologue going on in our minds—our mind drifts or jumps from thought to thought—so our inner critics can slip their messages in without our noticing. The next thing you know is that we've bought into their baloney and move further away from creating and expressing ourselves.

> *Today is Saturday. What a great day it will be. I get to spend two hours in my sewing room today. Right after I finish my coffee. And unload the dishwasher. And wipe down the counters. But today I am celebrating time to do with as I want. How glorious it will be. I wonder whether I should start by finishing the binding on that baby quilt or get right into the juicy improv quilt. Oh crumb, the bathrooms should be wiped as well. I should probably do that before I sew. It's never-ending, this need to clean. Why am I the only one who cleans around here? Why can't I get help so I can do my own stuff? It doesn't matter anyway. I don't know what I'm doing and I'm just going to mess it up. I'm not creative and I don't know who I'm fooling. Ah forget it; I'm not going to bother with any of that. Oh, look, there's a slice of banana bread left. I'll eat that and finish my coffee and maybe check out what's happening on Facebook.*

See what happens? We start the day with great intentions to go and create after we finish a couple chores. Our inner critic sees that as an opening and asks "How can you justify the time to sew when your house is still a mess?" The next thing you know, you are feeling resentment over the competing demands on your time and *WHAM!* your inner critic wades in with the knockout punch telling you that you are "not good enough" and "not creative at all." So we end up feeling dejected. More often than not, these negative messages lead us to avoidance activities like eating or playing on the internet instead of either *cleaning* or *creating*.

So what can we do? Learning to skillfully deal with our inner critics is a part of the creative process. The first thing is to be aware of negative messages as they happen. Think about the kinds of messages your gremlin tells you. It may be useful to write them down (making sure not to internalize them or get sucked into believing them) so that you can begin to understand their strategies. Then keep watch on your thoughts for those troublesome stories that your gremlin tells you. When you notice a gremlin thought happening you can think "I'm on to you, gremlin! You can stop right there!"

It can also be helpful to write positive affirmations that counter the negative messages from our inner critics. I often use two different pens and write a conversation between myself and my gremlin. My gremlin gets a gray or black pen for his negative messages and I use a pretty purple or turquoise pen for my positive responses. It's important that these affirmations be in your own voice. If you find it hard to write

a positive affirmation for yourself, imagine that you were writing one for a friend. Sometimes it can be easier to think positively about others than ourselves.

When flipping the negative messages from your inner critic into a positive affirmation, it is important to make them believable. Our mind is fabulous at arguing and looking for weaknesses in thinking, so try to create affirmations that your inner critic simply cannot argue against.

> **Gremlin** *Why bother trying that? You're only going to mess it up.*

> **You** *The best way to learn is to do. And even if it's terrible, I'll still learn something.*

Notice how this affirmation acknowledges the possibility that something might be *messed up*, but transforms such mistakes into learning opportunities.

> **Gremlin** *You'll never be as good as _____ .*

> **You** *I can't predict the future. She's worked hard to build her skills. If I work hard, I can get there too.*

Notice how this affirmation doesn't attempt to argue, but instead uses the other person as a role model. Anyone can work hard and improve their skills.

> **Gremlin**: *You're going to waste that fabric.*

> **You** *They always make more. And if they stop making fabric, I can cut up old clothing like my ancestors!*

And this affirmation is completely true! They will always make more fabric. And even if budget doesn't allow for all the fabric you can imagine, there are always creative ways to find more.

Sometimes it can be helpful to visualize our inner gremlins because then it gives us someone to talk back to. I've had two different ones over the years. My first gremlin looked just like my freshman English professor: short, bald, wearing glasses and a tweed coat with suede patches on the elbows, and carrying a leather briefcase. My current one, who I affectionately call Gremmy, is green and spiky, like Oscar the Grouch from Nightmareland. What does yours look like? Is he/she/it representative of someone from your past? An amalgamation of several people? Completely imaginary? Take time to form a strong visual image and then use that image when you talk back to it.

Learn to think of your inner critic as a harbinger of growth and change. Our gremlins stay quiet when we live our comfortable lives in our comfort zone. But when we try to stretch and grow and take on a new challenge, they come out. I look at my gremlin's temper tantrums as a sign that I am on the right path. The more he throws up a fuss, the more certain I am that I need to do that which I am afraid to do.

'Come to the edge.
'We can't. We're afraid.'
'Come to the edge.'
'We can't. We will fall!'
'Come to the edge.'
And they came.
And he pushed them.
And they flew.
 -Guillaume Apollinaire

Questions for Reflection about Inner Critics

You may wish to answer these questions in a separate notebook so you have more room to respond. Answer them all at one time or revisit them a little each day.

Does your inner critic talk to you? (If not, then Yippee! Run off and create with abandon!) What does it say? Make a list of the things you've heard. What messages is it trying to convey? What is it trying to get you to do? Or not do? How do these messages make you feel? What is your typical way of reacting when your inner critic pops up?

Can you visualize your inner critic? (It's fine if you can't.) What does it look like? What is it wearing? Is it carrying anything in particular? Is it situated in a certain environment? What does its voice sound like? You may wish to draw a picture of your critic. Don't worry about making it beautiful. Your critic might go crazy at this, which is all the more reason to give it a try. (If you're familiar with Harry Potter, boggarts are shape-shifting creatures that transform into the viewer's greatest fear. The best way to counter them is the *riddikulous* charm, which changes their appearance into something comical and weakens them.)

Think back on your visualization of your critic. Are there any clues that can help you identify where it comes from? Sometimes just knowing that we are carrying our fifth-grade art teacher or great-aunt or freshman English professor around with us can alleviate some of the negativity.

Look back over the list of messages. Can you counter each with a positive and affirming statement? If you are having a hard time thinking of one, imagine that a friend told you they felt that way about themselves. What would you say to them to counter their negative message?

What triggers your inner critic to pop up? Is it when you move into the unknown? When you try something new? When things don't go as planned? What would it mean to begin to envision your inner critic as a signpost for growth? What would it mean to move on despite your critic? Can you imagine the possibilities that come from no longer granting your critic the power to stop you?

Complete the following sentence as many times as you want. If I didn't let my inner critic stop me, I would _____. Let your imagination soar as you envision a life unfettered by the fears and constraints of your inner critic. How would your life look? How would you think about yourself differently?

Evaluating Your Own Work

Throughout this handbook, I will offer guidance on how to evaluate your stitches and lines as you work. So that you have a context for comparison, I will provide sample designs and motifs as the basis for evaluation. Remember that we all have our own personal style. Just because your stitching doesn't look like my sample doesn't mean that you are doing it wrong. In fact, strive not to copy my samples exactly, but make them yours—your interpretation, your voice, your style. I can't tell you how many times in class students put their own spin on the exercises and create designs with great energy and freshness. It inspires me to see with new eyes.

Some evaluation questions I provide will focus on the technical aspects of the design. And these questions will be based on my experience teaching lots of beginners over the years. The questions will have many gentle modifiers: are your stitches *relatively* consistent? Are your lines *mostly* straight? These modifiers are important to focus on. Free-motion quilting isn't about absolutes or perfection.

Some questions will focus on the artistic qualities of your stitching. These questions will help you find your inspiration by exploring the visual qualities of the design. What inspires you about the design you are stitching? How can you make it your own? What happens if you combined this with that?

Some evaluation questions may also encourage you to reflect on your experiences stitching—what is easier or harder? What comes naturally? How does it feel? Is your inner critic active? These reflective questions will remind you to focus on the process and how it feels. Knowing what feels natural and what feels hard can help you choose patterns that come from within and that represent your personal style or voice.

Developing the Skill to Estimate Distances, Sizes, and Heights

One skill that you will work on developing is your ability to eyeball distances and heights while free-motion quilting. This will allow you to quilt more efficiently without having to mark guidelines. Our eyes are actually quite good at being able to estimate distances and sizes. You may have the experience of being able to judge the accuracy of a ¼" seam allowance just by looking at it.

So to be able to estimate distances, sizes, and heights with relatively accuracy is a helpful skill to develop. That said recall that we have our own *consistent inconsistencies*, which will also appear in our estimations. These allow our personal mark-making style to show. And, with humans being natural pattern finders, when our consistent inconsistencies are apparent, viewers will still be able to recognize the underlying pattern. So balance developing your ability to estimate with your acceptance of your natural expression.

When an exercise has an element of eyeball estimation, I will provide a description of what to watch for as you estimate distances, sizes, and heights.

Exercise: Learning to Control Placement of Stitches

Objective

- o Learn to quilt stitches where you want them to be.
- o Practice moving the quilt in different directions without pivoting or rotating.
- o Begin estimating the length of lines and the distance between them.

You've just learned how to coordinate your foot pedal (needle) and hand speeds to make consistent, even stitches. Now you need to learn how to control your stitches—that is, how to plan where you want to quilt. Get a new practice quilt sandwich, if needed.

First, we will practice stitching and moving the quilt in different directions. When we free-motion quilt we don't want to have to pivot or turn the quilt to change directions because it is awkward and inefficient to stop and pivot when working on larger quilts. (Even though we are using smaller quilt sandwiches for learning, it's best to establish the good and necessary habit of never turning the quilt.)

We need to learn how to feel comfortable quilting from left to right as well as right to left. The same hold for quilting from top to bottom and from bottom to top. You may find that one direction feels most comfortable. That is normal. Practice both the comfortable and uncomfortable because that will help you become a better and more efficient quilter.

Grab your practice sketchbook and try the exercises on paper first. You'll read that for a lot of exercises because I truly believe that it makes learning easier to practice this way. Practicing an exercise on paper is more comfortable and the motion transfers to quilting. Once I start to feel a little bored with drawing, I switch from drawing on paper to stitching on the quilt. Boredom tells me that I have started to ingrain the drawing in my muscles and mind.

Moving the Quilt from Left to Right and Right to Left

You are going to first practice drawing and then stitching long lines (roughly 4"-5" long) moving from left to right and then right to left. When you reach the end of each line, drop down roughly ½" with a slight curve and stitch the next line back the way you came.

Try to make the lines parallel and roughly the same length. Try to make the lines an equal distance apart. Notice the curve at each end where you change direction.

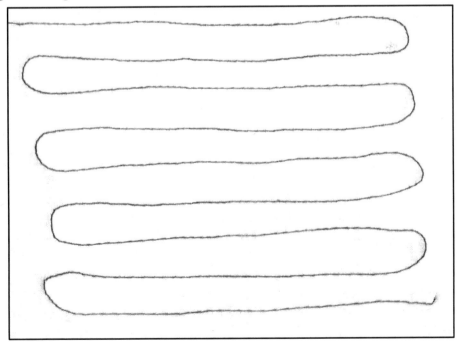

Eyeball Estimations

Begin developing your eye for estimation by trying to make the lines roughly straight, parallel, and the same distance apart from one another. Change directions in the same place, so that the curves stack on top of each other.

Gentle Evaluations

- ○ Are your lines *relatively* straight and parallel?
- ○ Are they *roughly* the same distance apart?
- ○ Are your curves *mostly* stacked atop each other?
- ○ Did stitching in one direction or the other feel more comfortable or natural?
- ○ Was your inner critic activated? How did you respond?

Moving the Quilt from Top to Bottom and Bottom to Top

Now try the same exercise, this time moving the quilt towards you and away from you (from top to bottom and from bottom to top). Practice in your sketchbook first. This may feel different from the side-to-side movements. That is fine and completely natural. Learning how different directions feel can help you design and plan your quilting in the future to feel comfortable and be aligned with your strengths.

Eyeball Estimations

Try to make the lines roughly straight, parallel, and the same distance apart. Change directions in the same place, so that the curves are aligned.

Gentle Evaluations

- ○ Are your lines *relatively* straight and parallel?
- ○ Are they *roughly* the same distance apart?
- ○ Are your curves *mostly* stacked atop each other?
- ○ Did stitching in one direction or the other feel more comfortable or natural?
- ○ Was your inner critic activated? How did you respond?

Variations: You can vary this basic movement pattern to create other quilting designs

Add bumpy waves as you move side to side.

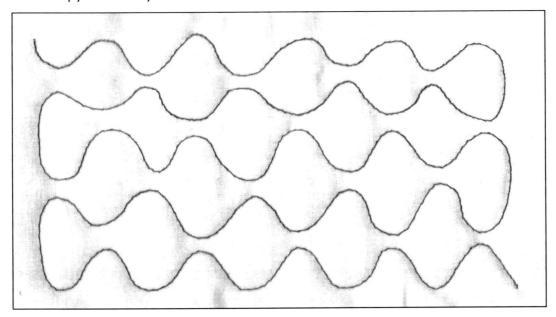

By alternating the widths between the lines, you can create a comb-like pattern.

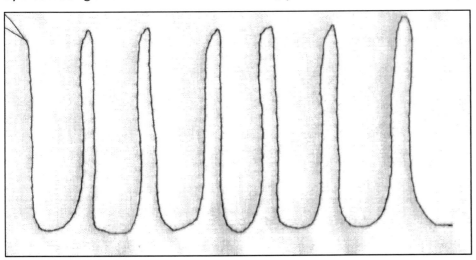

Or alternate the height to make peaky hills.

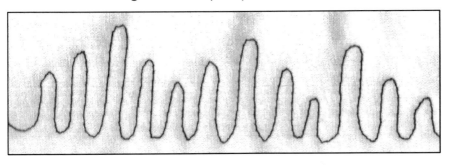

Exercise: Changing Directions More Often

Objectives

- Continue practicing moving the quilt in different directions, but change directions more frequently so that the lines are shorter.
- Continue practicing estimating height and width without marking lines or distances.
- Practice stitching smooth curves.

Now you are going to practice stitching the same design as the last exercise, only making the length of the lines shorter. This way you will be practicing changing directions more often.

Stitching From Left to Right and Right to Left with More Directional Changes

Begin with your sketchbook and draw elongated hairpin shapes from left to right. You are moving the quilt in a left to right direction for the rows but the movement for the hairpin shapes is up and down.

- Each hairpin should be roughly the same height. The actual height doesn't matter. **Imagine** lines at the top and bottom of the row and stitch the hairpins so that they fill that height. In the diagram below, these imaginary lines are the dashed lines. Note that you don't have to mark the lines. Instead, use this as practice estimating distance.
- Each hairpin should be roughly the same width. This is shown by the little barbells.

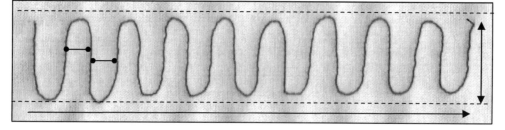

Shift between bottom-to-top and top-to-bottom.

Quilt moves in an overall left-to-right direction.

- After about 6" of hairpins, extend the down leg of the hairpin into the empty space below. Extend the line to about twice the height of your initial hairpins and add a little to allow for buffer space between the rows. Now stitch the same pattern from right to left.

- The little hairpin shapes should all be approximately the same height and width across the row. When you stitch the next row, you can use the row above to help you estimate width.

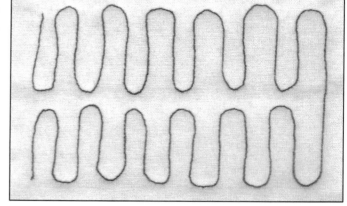

This will help the hairpins to stack on top of each other.

Stitch at least 5-7 rows atop each other. Stop and hold your sandwich at least an arm's length away. Look at the overall appearance, rather than focusing on the individual stitches or curves. Do you see what great texture is developing?

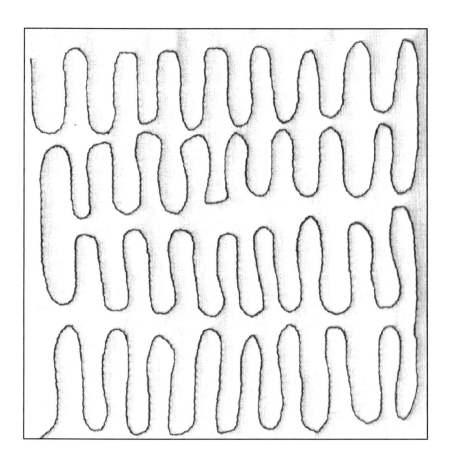

Gentle Evaluations

○ Your hairpin sizes and shapes may be different from the sample. This is fine! It shows your personal style and hand. Consider instead how your hairpins relate to one another and not how they compare to the sample.

○ Are your hairpins all *roughly* the same height and width? (That is, one hairpin looks similar to the next.)

○ Were you able to estimate how far down to drop at the end of each row?

○ Are your hairpins *relatively* stacked atop each other across rows?

○ Are your curves *mostly* smooth or are they somewhat jagged? The exercise "Assessing and Improving Your Curves" on page 42 will focus on smoothing out jagged curves.

○ Did your stitching change over the course of time? If so, how did it change?

Stitching From Bottom to Top and Top to Bottom with More Directional Changes

Grab your sketchbook again. This time, draw and then stitch your elongated hairpin shapes so they are oriented sideways and stack from top to bottom and then bottom to top.

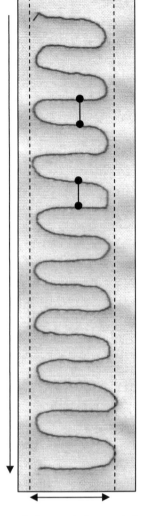

Quilt moves in an overall top-to-bottom direction.

o Each hairpin should be roughly the same width. **Imagine** lines at the left and right of the row and stitch the hairpins so that they fill that width. The dashed lines show these imaginary lines. Note that you don't need to mark the lines. Instead, you can practice estimating distance, which will help you become a more efficient quilter.

o Each hairpin should be approximately the same height. These are shown by the little barbell shapes.

o After about 6" take the final right-to-left leg of the hairpin and extend it into the empty space to the right. Extend the line to the right about twice the width of your initial hairpins and add a little to allow for buffer space between the columns. Now stitch the same pattern from bottom to top.

Shift between left-to-right and right-to-left to create the hairpins.

o The little hairpin shapes should all be approximately the same width across the columns. When you stitch the next column, you can use the column to the left to help you estimate width. This will help the hairpins align with one another.

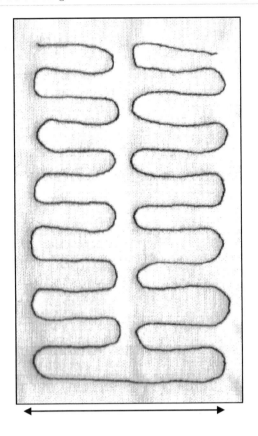

If the width of the first row is 1", then extend the final line of the row to the right about 2¼" to allow for the width of the second row and ¼" of buffer space.

Gentle Evaluations

○ Your hairpin sizes and shapes may be different from the sample. This is fine! It shows your personal style and hand. Consider how your hairpins relate to one another and not how they compare to the sample.

○ Are your hairpins all *roughly* the same height and width? (One hairpin looks similar to the next.)

○ Were you able to estimate how far down to stitch to the right at the end of each column?

○ Are your hairpins *relatively* stacked atop each other across columns?

○ Are your curves *mostly* smooth or are they somewhat jagged? The next exercise will focus on smoothing out jagged curves.

○ Did your stitching change over the course of time? If so, how did it change? What happened?

Exercise: Assessing and Improving Your Curves

Objective

o   To assess and improve the smoothness of your curves.

Being able to quilt curves that are smooth is important to your learning. For some, curves come easily, but for others, a few tweaks to your technique can lead to great improvement. Many, many quilting designs have curves so you'll want to learn to stitch smooth curves in all directions.

Begin by stitching a row of loopy curves. Stitch in the direction that you feel most comfortable. For most people, this is stitching from left to right. Try clockwise and counterclockwise curves.

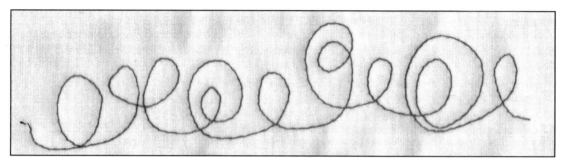

Repeat the loopy curves in the opposite direction—from right to left. Then try stitching curves from top to bottom. You can change the pattern up for fun. Play with different curve designs. What the design looks like isn't as important as what the curves look like.

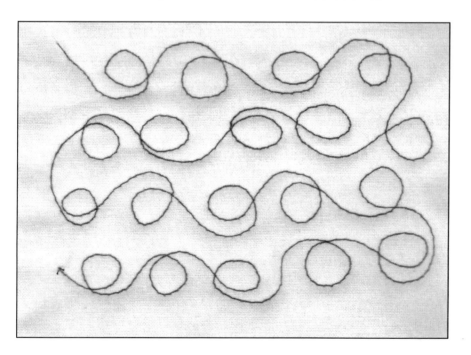

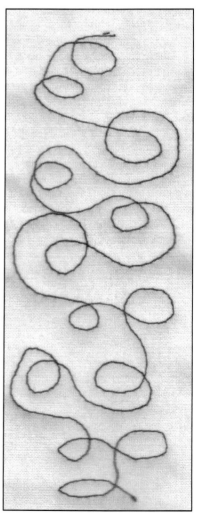

Gentle Evaluations

o Once you've stitched your loops, evaluate the smoothness of your curves.
o Are *most* of your curves *relatively* smooth? If so, that is fantastic. Your curves will continue to even out as you practice.
o Is there a pattern to where your curves are not smooth? Do they tend to appear on the same part of the curve? Or on the same part of the design? Or when you are moving a certain direction?
o Are you seeing eyelashes, where the bobbin thread is being pulled to the top of the quilt, on the outer edge of the curve?
o Are your stitches consistent around the entirety of the curve? Do they get smaller as you go around the outside of the curve?

After evaluating your curves, you can begin to adjust your stitching to improve the smoothness of your curves.

Glide the quilt sandwich around the curve

One common thing that beginners do is force the quilt sandwich around the curve. The motion of controlling and guiding the quilt smoothly under the needle takes practice. Watch for herky-jerky motions when changing direction in a curve. If you've ever ice skated or skied, then you have experienced smoothly going around curves. The idea is to glide smoothly through the curve. Jerky or forced motions lead to tripping or falling over. The same thing happens with stitching. If you force your way around the curve, you can create jagged curves.

Avoid pushing or pulling too fast around the curve

Eyelashes, where it looks like the bobbin thread is being pulled to the top, represent pulling or pushing the fabric too fast as you go around the curve. In this case, your sewing machine can't keep up with the speed at which you are moving the quilt and the tension goes awry. Maintain a consistent speed as you stitch through the curve. If this problem continues, you may want to have your machine serviced. Let the repair technician know that you are seeing tension problems when free-motion-stitching curves and they can adjust the tension on your machine.

Coordinating hand speed and foot pedal speed

You may find that your stitches are smaller when you are going around a curve—this is often because when we go around curves we slow down our hands to maneuver around the curve, but maintain our foot pedal speed. Think about slowing your hands and foot pedal speed in conjunction with one another so you have even stitches all around the curve or point. This is like driving around a sharp curve, where you slow down the speed of the car to stay on the road. So as you approach portions of the design where your hands slow down, you should slow your foot pedal speed accordingly.

Remember to Relax

The most important thing that you can do when free-motion quilting curves (or anything for that matter) is to relax into what you are doing. Relaxed and confident movements create smoother and more graceful lines than tight and questioning movements.

When you're learning, even if you aren't quite confident yet, it can be useful to pretend that you are. Relax into the movements. Watch your shoulders—they tend to rise up near our ears when we are stitching. This causes us to grip the quilt tightly and force the movements. Imagine sandbags resting gently on your shoulders as you quilt. This can help you keep shoulders down and relaxed.

Periodically stop, get up, and move around. Release the tension from your upper body—shake out your hands, wiggle your shoulders, flap your arms. Let yourself wiggle and wriggle and move the blood through your body.

Take three deep breaths—inhaling in confidence and belief and exhaling tension and worry. Find your relaxed center. Take a moment to visualize successful quilting. Imagine yourself moving gracefully along with the quilt. Feel how smoothly you can glide around curves, like a bird swooping and soaring.

Then quilt some curves and see how it feels.

On Knowing When Enough is Enough

Sometimes when we are quilting things just don't go our way. The needle breaks. The bobbin runs out in the middle of a line. We spill our coffee. And we try a new design and just can't get it. We try again and again and just start to feel frustrated.

Sometimes it's okay to let it go and say "Tomorrow is another day." A good night's sleep always helps.

Just remember to return.

Always return.

Exercise: Beginning with Meandering

Objectives

- o Understand how meandering (and other background, overall designs) are really about understanding how to fill space.

- o Begin to develop your own meandering style.

So you have practiced creating consistent stitches, changing directions frequently, and stitching smooth curves. Now it is time to try meandering, which teaches you great things about how to fill space and about making art decisions.

Meandering is one of the most common free-motion patterns and is frequently used for backgrounds or as an overall design. (Stippling is another word that is used interchangeably to describe this pattern, but technically stippling refers to very small micro-quilting, often as close as ¼" apart. Meandering refers to the larger-scale pattern that we will be stitching here.)

The trick is to create shapes that look like puzzle pieces, fairly consistent in shape and size, but not predictable in path or direction. You will develop your own style of meandering that will be unique and individual, like your handwriting. The important thing is that the curves and bumps not be predictable. You shouldn't be able to look at your meandering and see a pattern. It should just look like overall texture.

Both the samples below show meandering that's not quite right. The one on the left is not quite consistent enough for meandering, although, it would make a lovely pattern on its own. The sample on the right is too predictable. It is similar to some of our practice exercises and would also make a great background on its own.

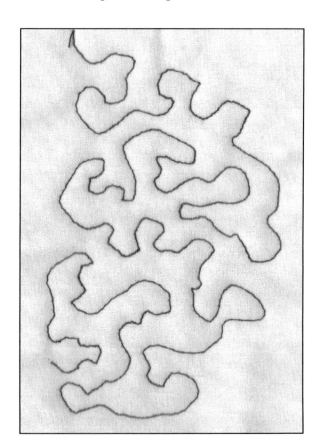
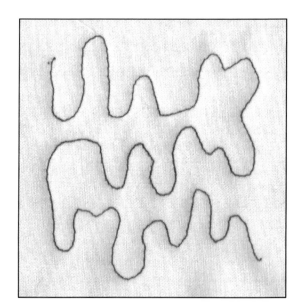

Meandering is consistent but not predictable. As the top picture shows, the general shapes of meandering are roughly the same size, but the path is not predictable.

The trick to making meandering fill the space randomly is to understand that you are traveling a *wandering path that wanders*. There are two levels of wandering.

The first level of wandering is how you fill space—not in a series of predictable rows, but in a path that wanders around. In the bottom picture, the dashed lines show the general direction changes involved in filling the space. Notice that that the dashed path wanders and changes directions as it fills the box.

The meandering quilting (solid stitching line) shows the second level of wandering. Notice how the stitching moves in the general direction indicated by the dashed lines, but that there is a lot of wandering along the way.

It's like following a highway through the mountains. The road may be called 56 West, but you may end up traveling north, south, or even east as the road wanders through the mountain path—and all the while you are ultimately heading west.

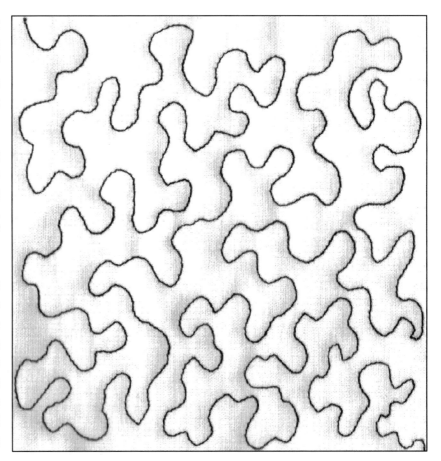

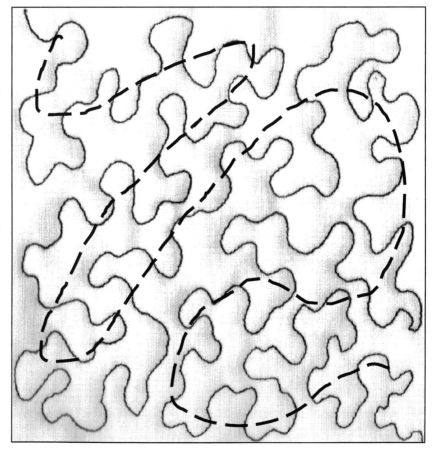

Here the general direction of space filling has been isolated. You can imagine that there are an infinite number of ways a wandering path can sit on this dashed path.

At the same time, there are an infinite number of ways that a wandering path can fill space.

Take a moment and doodle a wandering path that follows the dashed lines.

If you find yourself making the same shape in the same direction twice, then you need to change direction.

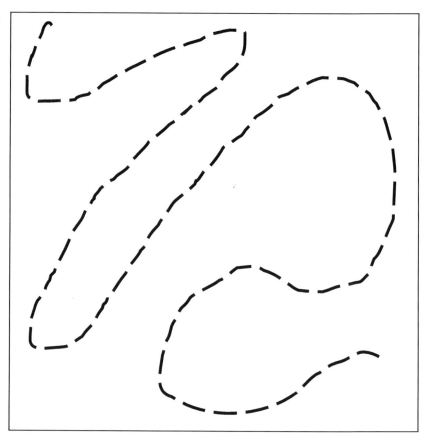

Make a few photocopies of the next page for tracing. Tracing this will help you become familiar with the movements and shapes of meandering. When tracing, use large arm movements. We normally trace using small wrist movements, but to more accurately practice the whole-body movements of quilting, use larger movements to make your marks on paper.

This sample is a medium-large meandering size, which will allow you to begin with larger movements. As you begin to become comfortable with the concept of meandering, then you can refine it and stitch on a smaller scale.

You may also want to take a moment and explore the general wandering path that fills the space. Notice how it is different from the previous example, but gives the impression of looking the same.

These quarter-page samples show four different sizes for meandering. You can photocopy this page and practice tracing. Each sample starts in the upper left and ends in the lower right.

Take a couple of pages in your sketchbook and divide them into quarters. Choose your starting and ending points and try drawing your own meandering designs in each quarter.

Once you are starting to feel comfortable with the decision-making and space-filling aspects of meandering, then try quilting your practice sandwiches. Draw a 5" square on your quilt sandwich. You are going to quilt the meandering design in the square. This is similar to quilting in smaller spaces on a quilt. Decide where you will start and stop your quilting line.

Start

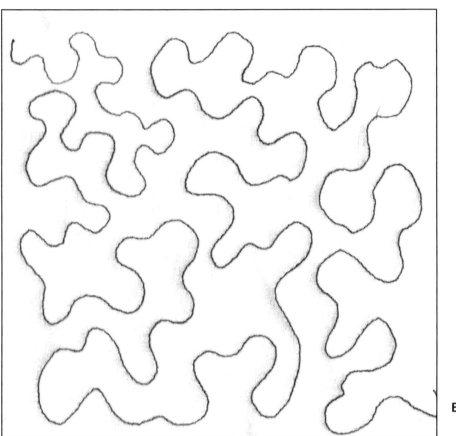

End

Eyeball Estimations

o   Before you begin stitching, get clear on where you want to start and end your quilting line. Envision the overall path you will take to fill the space as you move from the starting point to the end point. Remember to wander as you follow your wandering path.

Gentle Evaluations

o   Does your meandering look like a wandering path that wanders? Or are you finding that you are stitching in rows? Try to remember never to stitch in the same direction for more than two or three bumps. Direction changes help meandering appear more random.

o Are you getting caught in corners and having to cross lines to complete the space? Crossing lines isn't the end of the world, but you can resolve this by envisioning your path before you stitch, including your starting and ending points.

o Everyone has a unique style, so your meandering might not look exactly like the samples provided. That is perfectly fine. In many ways, meandering is just like handwriting—we all have our unique ways of making marks. The important thing is to fill space in a random pattern that is consistent without being predictable.

o Here are two other styles of meandering. One has a slightly jagged feel that reminds me of islands and rivers. The other has long, smooth fingerlike shapes. Notice how they fill the space in a consistent, but not predictable way. They are still wandering paths that wander.

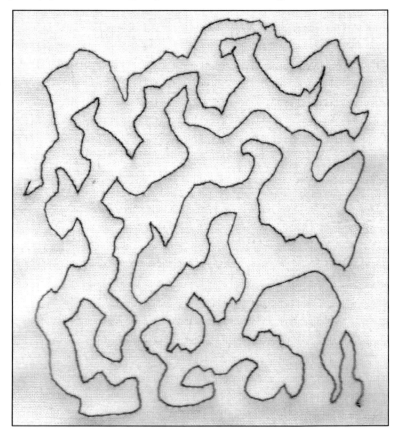

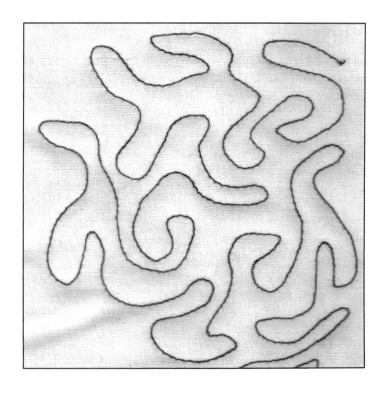

Exercise: Modifying Basic Meandering with Ribbons

One nice addition to a wandering line is to turn it into a twisted ribbon. This works really well with larger-scale meandering with gentle curves to give it more presence. Begin with one meandering line then add a second line of stitching parallel to it. The trick to making this look like a twisted ribbon is to **stitch the second line so that it is always outside the outer curve of the first line**. The second picture shows how the new line always sits outside the outer curve of the first stitching line. Notice how the second line crosses over the first at the midpoint of the curve, which is about where an outside curve becomes an inside curve.

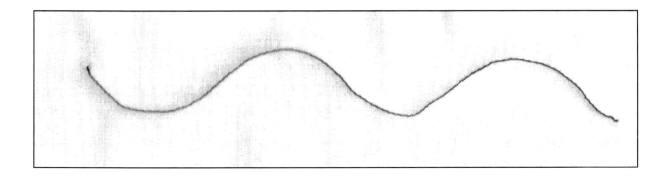

Midpoint where the inside curve becomes an outside curve and vice versa.

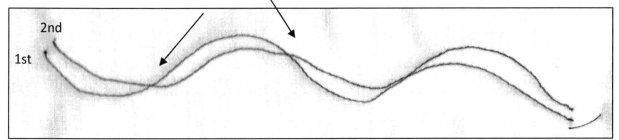

Eyeball Estimations

○ Make sure that the second meandering line is always located outside the curve of the first.
○ Cross over the first line at the midpoint, which is where the outside curve turns into an inside curve.

Gentle Evaluations

○ Do your quilting lines resemble a twisted ribbon?
○ Are you feeling comfortable determining when to switch from the outside of the curve to the inside of the curve?

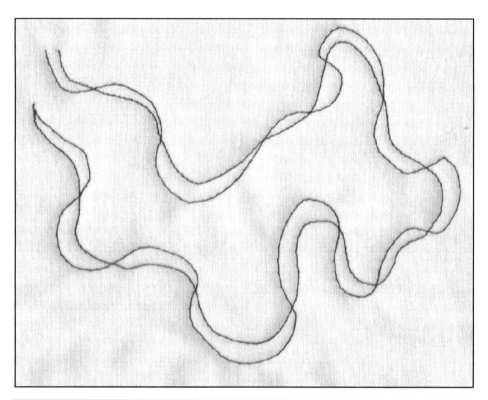

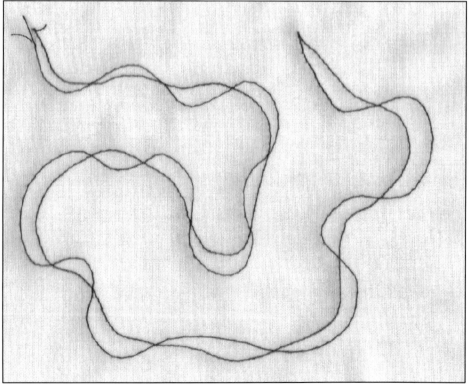

Exercise: Feeling Loopy?

Some people are a little *loopy*. That's more than okay—it's what makes life fun! What that means in this case is that some people have a tendency to add loops while they are meandering. That is perfectly fine and shows that you are beginning to add your own style to your work. You can also play with loops in other quilting designs, such as rows or columns. Here are several loopy patterns for your inspiration.

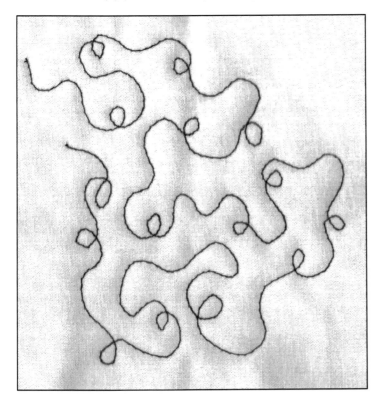

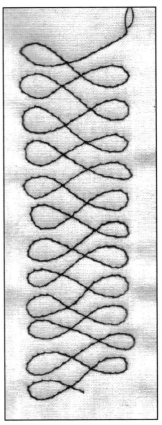

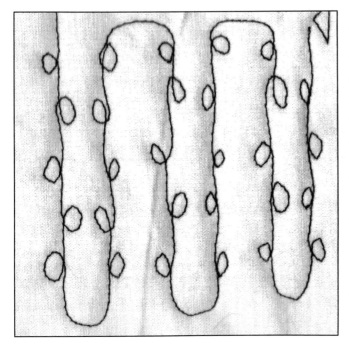

Gentle Evaluations

○ Do loops feel natural or do they feel hard? Either is great. It's all part of discovering your natural rhythm as a free-motion quilter. For example, loops do not feel natural to me, but I've included them as inspiration for those who may find them comfortable.

○ Are your loops all going in the same direction? Changing the direction of loops so that some turn clockwise and others counterclockwise can help them look more random, if that is what you are looking for.

Exercise: Adding Motifs to Meandering

Once you have mastered the basic rhythm of meandering, you can enhance it by adding motifs. Choose motifs that work with your fabric or to add a subtle message to your quilting. Add hearts to say "I love you" or stars to connect with cosmic possibilities. Or add flowers and leaves to create the lush growth of a garden. You'll need to become familiar with stitching motifs from all different starting positions, like upside-down leaves or horizontal hearts. Here are the tips for how to add motifs.

o   Add the motif to the **outside of a curve**, not the inside of a curve. If you add one to the inside curve every now and then, no problem, but lots of motifs added to the inside curves often make the design feel trapped or crowded.

o   Add the motif to the **midpoint of the outside curve**.

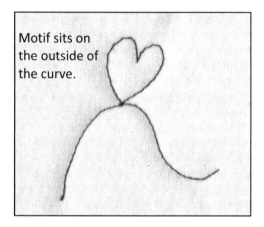
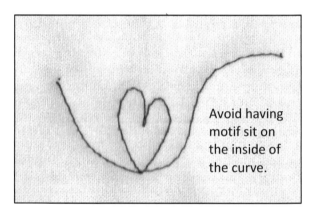

o   Always **add motifs in the same direction as you were traveling**. At left below, you were moving clockwise around the curve so you want to go clockwise to create the heart. Note that it looks like the heart is sitting on the curve.

o   Never cross over into the other direction. At right below, you were moving clockwise around the curve and then counter-clockwise into the heart. Note that the heart and curve form an X-intersection.

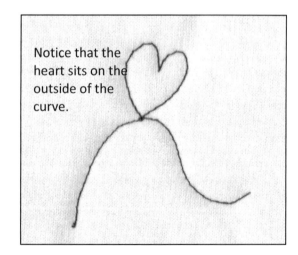
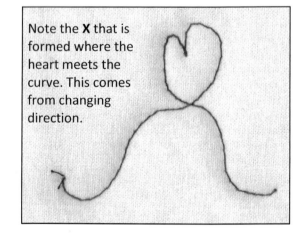

Eyeball Estimations

Space the frequency of adding the motif evenly. I usually add motifs every two or three bumps—always on the outside curves. And so that they look randomly scattered, make sure that they are oriented in all directions—upside-down, right-side up, sideways, diagonally.

Remember Our Minds are Great Pattern Finders

Remember our minds' natural tendencies to look for patterns. This is a great benefit for learning. Your motifs don't all have to look perfect—as long as some resemble what they are supposed to be then the mind fills in the blanks and says "Hey, look at all those stars!" Or hearts. Or leaves. As you stitch, you will see that some of the hearts or stars may look a little funny, but since the majority are recognizable the mind sees them all as hearts or stars.

Bumpy Patterns

The hearts and three-petal flower that follow resemble each other, with a slight difference. The heart is made of two bumps, where the separating line is short. The flower is made of three bumps and the separating lines between the petals go all the way down to touch to top of the curve.

Hearts...

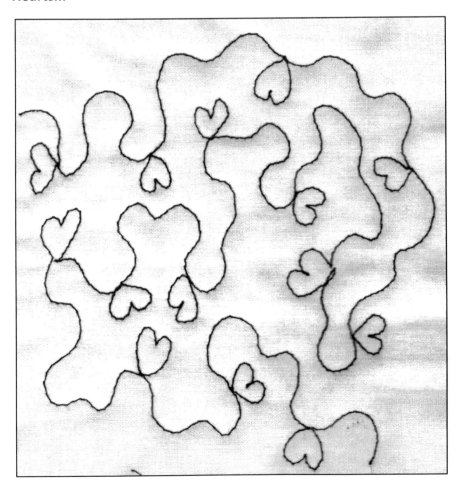

Flowers….

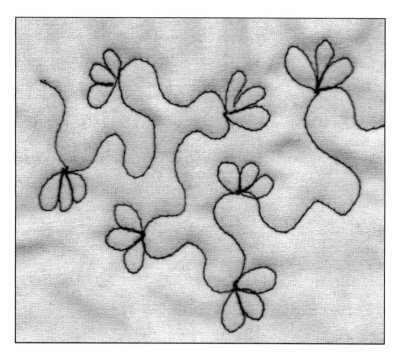

Pointed Patterns

To make sharp points, as on the stars and leaves, you need to take the slightest pause at the change of direction. Too long a pause and you'll cause stitches to build up. Too short a pause and you'll end up with slightly curved points. I like to think of it as a quick beat. Stitch, stitch, PAUSE, stitch, stitch.

Here's a refresher on the steps for drawing a five-pointed star. Practice drawing stars in all directions, even upside-down.

Stars...

Notice how the stars are dancing all over the meandering line. You'll need to be able to draw stars starting from any point to add them to meandering in a random way.

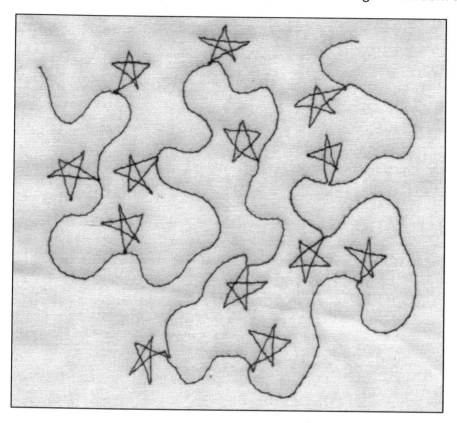

Leaves...

To stitch a leaf, begin at the base of the leaf and stitch upwards to the tip, pause for a brief moment, then stitch down to the base. The leaf should look like a candle-flame. The pause before you change direction gives a sharp tip to the leaf. Once you have returned to the base of the leaf, take a short trip up the middle of the leaf and then back down, creating the vein. On your trip back, follow the initial vein or wander alongside it. The important thing the vein does is help the brain recognize the candle-flame shape as a leaf.

Gentle Evaluations

- o Are your motifs sitting on the outside of the curve?
- o Are they scattered evenly around the quilting design?
- o Do you create the motifs in the same direction as you were traveling around the curve, or do you change direction and have little X's form at the intersection of motif and curve?
- o Do you have sharp points on stars and leaves?
- o Are most of your motifs recognizable? Remember, our brains are natural pattern detectors, so if most of your motifs are recognizable, the ones that you think look a little funny will also be recognizable in context. Thanks, brain!

Exercise: Practice Stitching Motifs in Rows

You can practice creating recognizable motifs by stitching them in rows and columns. These also make great border, background, or sashing fills. You can run them vertically or horizontally. You can also stitch them so the motif appears on alternating sides of the central line, which gives you practice stitching them in different directions. Practice rows are a great way to experiment with creating other motif designs.

Hearts....

Rows of hearts add a feel of whimsy and love. Notice that the pointy end of the heart rests on the line and does not cross.

Try stitching them right-side up and upside-down. This will help you stitch them in different directions when meandering.

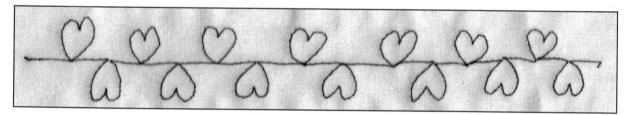

Stars...

Notice the stars in these rows appear to be dancing. This is because only one leg of the star is touching the line. Each star is oriented slightly differently, which makes them appear to move.

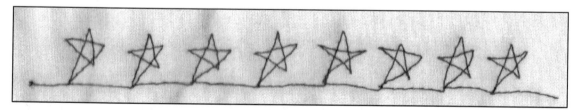

To review, the trick to having sharp star points (or sharp points or corners of any kind) is to take a short pause at each sharp change of direction. It's a two-stitch pause, where the needle makes two stitches in the same spot, which makes for sharp points. Too long a pause leads to too many stitches in a hole and forms a thread clump on the back of the quilt.

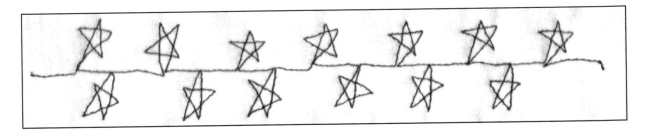

Leaves...

Notice how the up and down movement of each leaf resembles a candle flame. Just like making star points, remember to take a short pause at the top of the leaf to create a sharp leaf tip. Then travel up and down the same center of the leaf shape to create the vein. Leaves growing along both sides of a row resemble a vine. Remember that no two leaves in nature are alike.

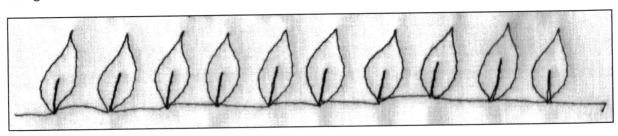

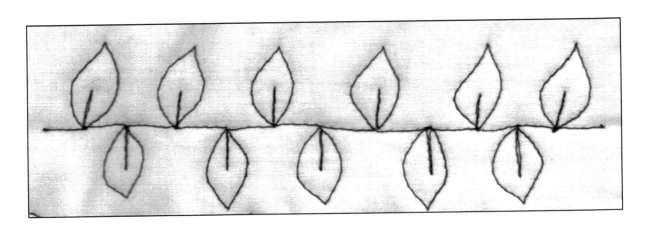

Variations on a Theme

The next series of row motifs will show you how some simple changes can spark a variety of different ideas. Use the examples for inspiration and to spark your own imagination. Have your sketchbook and practice sandwiches next to you and create your own designs.

Seed pods...

Seed pods start with a larger upside-down teardrop shape. Add a smaller teardrop inside.

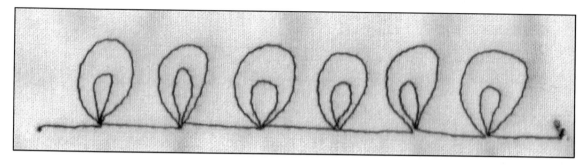

Change the proportions of the outer and inner pods. Stitch the pods on both sides of a row.

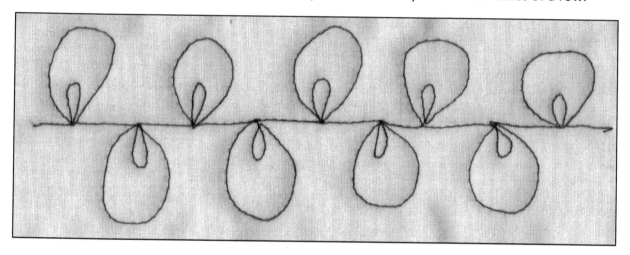

You can also add two inner seeds.

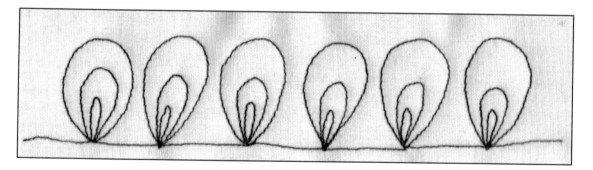

Or alternate the size and height of the seed pods. Short and fat alternates with tall and skinny.

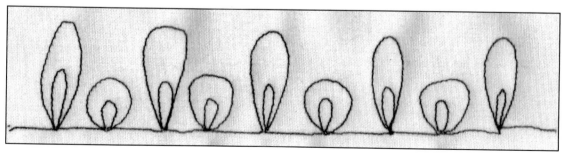

Shapes...

You can add shapes to a line in a couple of ways. They can sit on the line like building blocks.

Or the shapes can stand separate from the line, but attached with a short stem. These almost look like abstract trees or flowers.

Add smaller inner shapes on short stems.

Here, seed pods are added to a line using the short stem method. Notice the variation of heights and sizes. Some have two circles and others only one. Maybe they look like abstract trees.

Flowers...

These are super simple three-petal flowers: all the pretty flowers lined up in rows.

Alternating flowers on both sides of the row.

Here, the petals become pointy and a small inner pod is added.

Sharper and pointier petals (four of them) with an inner pod.

Seed pods with triangle borders become flowers with bite!

Triangles....

Triangles along a row create a sharp graphic design.

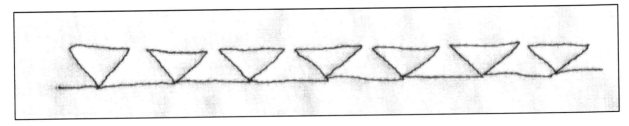

Alternate them on both sides for more interest.

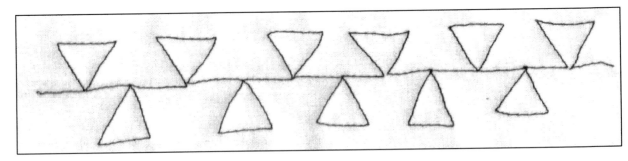

Or add a second triangle inside to make triangular seed pods.

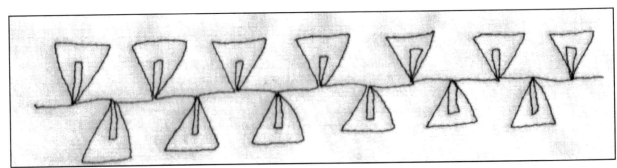

Gentle Evaluations

- Are your curves smooth where they need to be smooth?
- Are your points sharp where they need to be sharp?
- Are you spacing your motifs along the row relatively evenly?
- Is it easier to stitch the motif in one direction or the other?
- Are you remembering to celebrate your *consistent inconsistencies?*

Next Steps

Are you starting to see the infinite possibilities available for designing your own motifs? You can change the size, proportion, number, or height. You can alternate motifs on both sides of a row. Combine ideas and make the designs your own.

Exercise: Multi-Pass Rows

Interesting row designs can also be created in a couple of passes. This allows for space between the motifs and creates an interesting central spine. Start at one end and quilt all the motifs on top. Then change direction at the end of the row and quilt the motifs upside down.

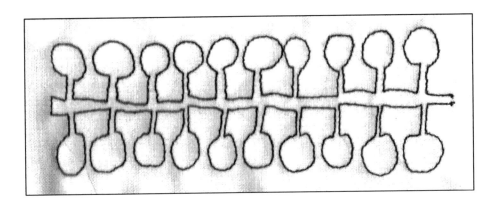

Exercise: More Complex Continuous Designs

There is a little trick to stitching more complex continuous designs like the ones that follow.

Start with the central line and extend it to the far side of the shape you want to create. In this example, you can see that the central line extends through the space of the circle. Complete the shape and then extend the center line to the far side of the next shape. Here, you can see the start of the rectangle.

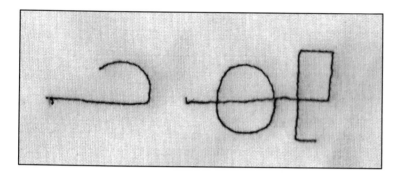

Complete this process for an alternating row of circles and rectangles along a central line.

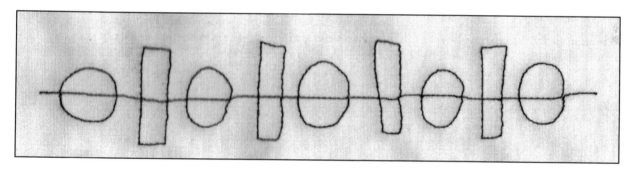

You can do the same for shapes inset in larger shapes. Here, begin on the central line and extend it to the far side of the smaller shape you want to create. Complete the smaller shape then continue with central line to the far side of the bigger shape. Complete the bigger shape and continue.

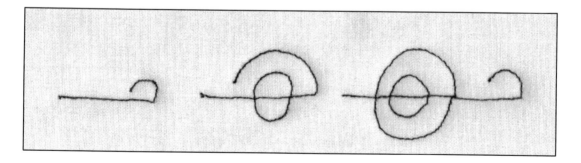

Complete this process for circles in circles along a central line.

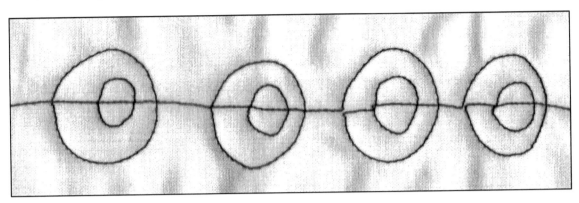

You can use this idea for other shapes, such as rectangles or diamonds.

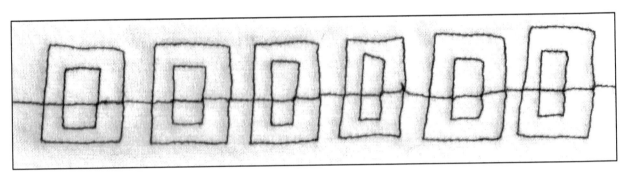

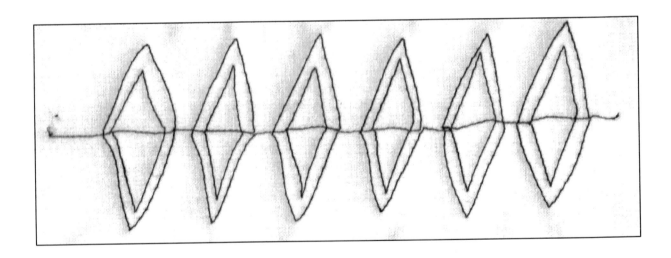

You can use this basic principle with more complex designs, such as this flower and leaf motif. Begin with two leaves and then stitch to the circular center of the blossom. Stitch a circle. When you reach the starting point of the circle, begin to stitch petals around the flower center.

When you get back to the start with your petals, then you will travel along the center line, around the flower center, and then out between or on top of the petals. Stitch two more leaves and repeat.

You can use this same basic strategy with different types of leaves and flowers. Experiment, play, and create your own pattern to express your individual visual language.

Gentle Evaluations

- Are you feeling inspired by any of these complex row designs?
- Have you begun to doodle designs of your own?
- Are you having fun?
- Are you remembering to play, explore, and record any ideas you have in your quilt sketchbook?

Exercise: Angled Meanders and Background Fills

So far we have been focusing on curved meanders. You can also create meander-style backgrounds that have angles rather than curves. The basic architecture of them is the same— you fill the space in the same way with a wandering path that wanders—only now you are seeking to create corners and points. So instead of trying to have smooth changes of direction that glide around curves, you want to have sharp changes of direction that lead to points and angles.

Remember that to create a sharp point or corner, you need to take a short pause at the place where you will change directions.

Try some based on 90 angles...

Or other angles...

Loopy squares...

Or loopy triangles...

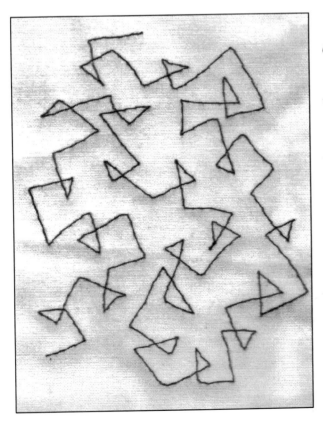

Gentle Evaluations

o Are you filling the space in a wandering way?

o Are your points sharp where they need to be sharp? Are you remembering the two-stitch pause?

Things that Feel Natural vs. Things that Feel Hard

As you begin to learn free-motion quilting, you will find that some motions, lines, or designs feel more comfortable than others. This again relates to your own personal style and is normal. For example, about 15% of the students who take my class are *loopy*. No, that doesn't mean they are cuckoo, it just means that when they learn a new pattern, like meandering, they always want to make loops. It's their natural style to add loops to their lines and curves. I always encourage them to go with it and devise their own meandering style that uses loops.

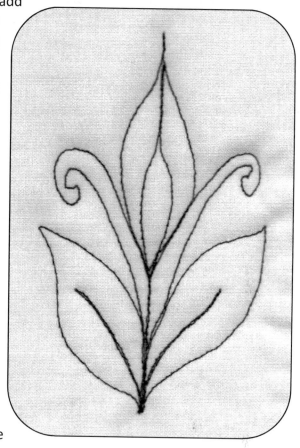

And you can do the same. Take a moment and reflect upon what motions and lines feel comfortable and seek out other patterns that have similar movements. Once you begin to identify the lines and shapes that feel natural, you can play with them in different combinations to create your own personal quilting marks.

If there are designs that feel hard, you can also take time to work with them to see if they become more comfortable with practice.

For me, botanical shapes like leaves and vines feel very comfortable, but feathers challenge me greatly. Even though they would seem to have similar forms, I find the experiences of stitching them to be very different. So I challenged myself while making a large Rag Quilt to quilt all the yellow squares with feathers (1/12 of the total). While I found that my skills at stitching feathers improved, they never felt comfortable to me—not in the way that botanicals do.

But more than that, I realized that feathers are not part of my visual language. Although I love to see feathers on others' quilts, they are not part of how I see the world. And so I released the need to use and master them and chose instead to continue to work with designs that move me and come from my own personal voice.

Allow yourself to explore your own interests and perspectives and discover your own visual language.

Exercise: Stitching Natural Elements of Water, Fire, Earth, and Sky

Look to nature for inspiration. Here are several background designs that are inspired by natural elements of water, fire, earth, and sky.

*Water....*Imagine elongated meanders that are spread out to look like reflections in the water or gently rippling water.

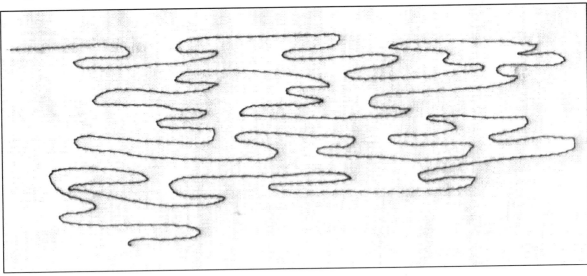

Or flames....

Dynamic flame shapes echo the energetic movement of a fire.

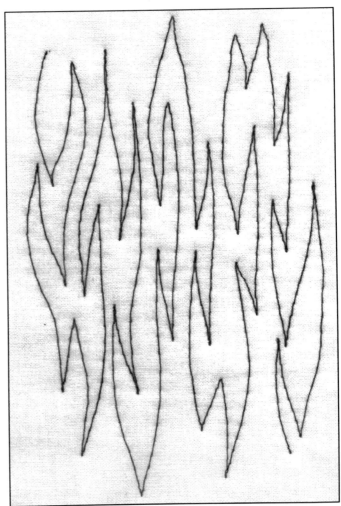

Or wood grain...

Parallel lines interrupted by knots simulate woodgrain.

Or clouds.....

A cloudy sky is made of overlapping fluffy pillows inspires this background.

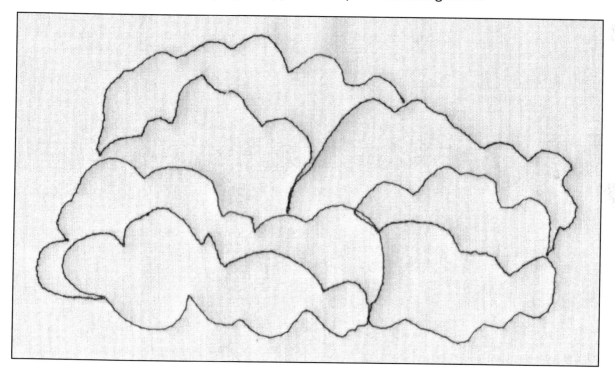

Or pebbles…

Pebbles make a beautiful pattern, but it does take a while and uses a lot of thread because of the backtracking that is necessary to create each individual pebble and then travel to the next pebble space.

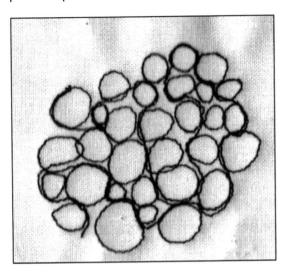

Or scales…

Scales can fill background space with an organic texture.

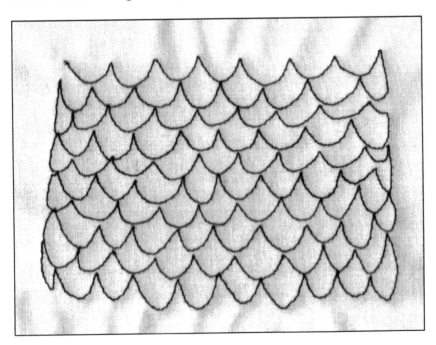

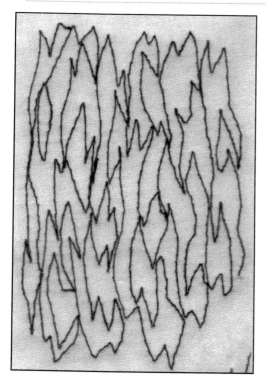

Or tree bark...

Spend time exploring the trees in your neighborhood. Can you translate the texture into a visual design?

Here, I've been inspired by the rough bark of our Southern Pine.

Or natural growth...

How do things grow? What patterns can you find in the weeds in a ditch or in the wildflowers in a field?

Here, I took my inspiration from an old sketch of weeds standing in a ditch after the frost.

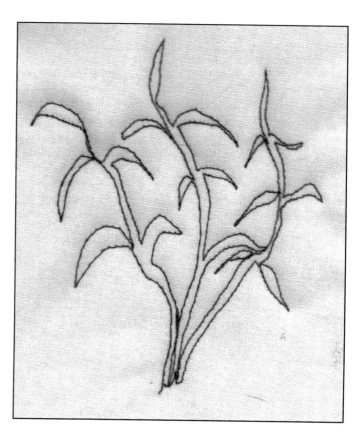

Gentle Evaluations

○ Which of these patterns feel comfortable to you? Which feel awkward?
○ What patterns in nature inspire you? What always catches your eye and moves your creative spirit? How can you translate nature's inspiration into a continuous quilting motif?
○ Is there any overlap between the patterns that feel comfortable and the natural patterns that inspire you? Often the things that inspire us are part of our visual language. Play with your inspirations and come up with your own variations.

Exercise: Spiraling In and Back Out

Other fills that work well are spirals. You can spiral any shape. Begin by spiraling in, but leave the pathway in TWICE as wide as you want it to be so that you can spiral back out comfortably.

At left, there is plenty of room to spiral back out comfortably. But in the picture at right, the path inwards is too narrow to spiral back out comfortably.

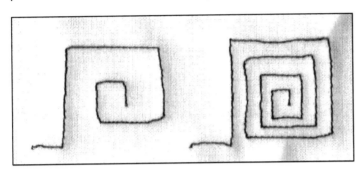

This pattern started in the bottom left and worked right and the spirals are clockwise. The trick is the second row, which travels from right to left and spirals counterclockwise. Practice spiraling in both directions to make background fills like this. Remember that the brain loves consistent inconsistencies and finding patterns.

Spiral in with circular paths.

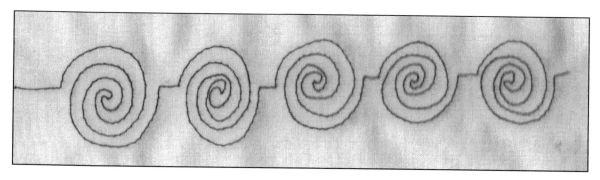

Spiral waves create the feeling of the ocean and moving water.

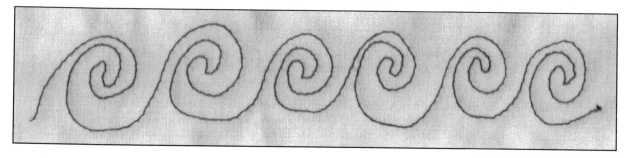

Spiral diamonds have an exotic feel.

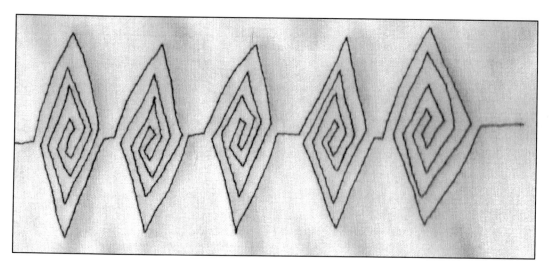

Here leaf or flame shapes spiral in and out. These would make a great background fill because you can nest the second row in the spaces left by the first row.

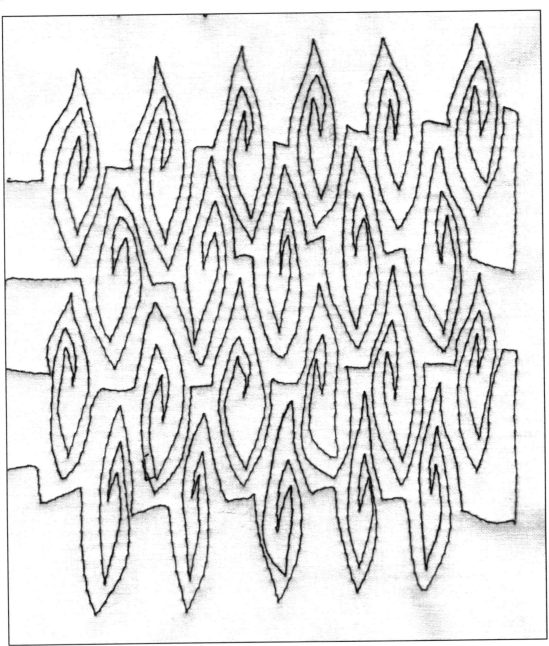

Gentle Evaluations

- o Did you remember to leave yourself enough room to spiral back out?
- o Does spiraling in one direction feel more comfortable than spiraling in the other?
- o Are you allowing yourself to be a beginner and remembering that we all have our consistent inconsistencies that represent our unique mark-making style?

Exercise: What's Your Name? (aka Write on Your Quilt)

You've been writing your name and the alphabet since elementary school—you are very familiar with the movements of cursive writing. You don't have to think about how to connect the letters F U N to spell fun because you have been writing it for so long. You can leverage this muscle memory and instinctive knowledge by quilting cursive letters and words. It may take a little practice to translate the movements of writing into quilting, but the transition can happen quickly. And then you can really build your skills making consistent stitches and placing stitches where you want them to be.

There are a couple of lower case letters that require an adjustment in how you create them—the letters "t" and "x" with their crosses and the letters "i" and "j" with their dots.

For the letter "t" you will stitch up to where you want the cross located, then stitch the left the half the cross, return to the center, stitch up as high as you want the "t", stitch down to the cross, stitch the right half of the cross, return to the center, and then carry on.

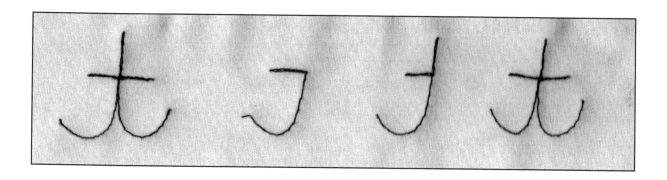

For the letter "x," you are going to quilt it in a similar manner. Begin with the curve that leads to the "x" then stop at the place where you would add the cross. Stitch down and to the left and then travel back up and to the right to make the cross. Stitch back to the center and finish out the "x."

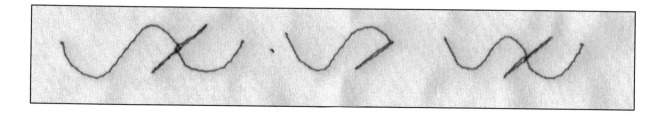

For the letters "i" and "j," you have two options. One is to stitch the dot as a little circle connected at the top of the letter. The other is to go back at the end and add each dot as a separate little circle. Each has pros and cons. Quilting the dot as a connected circle is more efficient, while stitching them as separate dots looks more like the actual letters. Give both a try and see how you like them.

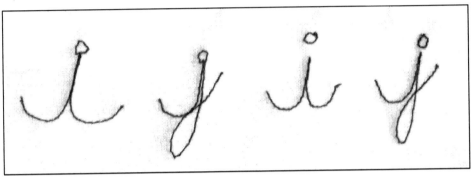

Try stitching the entire lower-case alphabet to begin to build your comfort with translating your automatic writing movements into quilting. You may wish to draw a line with a chalk wheel or just eyeball a straight line on which to quilt your letters.

Once you become comfortable quilting letters and words, it can be a fun way to add messages to your quilts. Think about adding words, quotes, messages of love, song lyrics, or poetry. You can embed the label in the quilt itself by adding your name, date, and location.

To travel from one word to the next, just stitch a line along the bottom.

Gentle Evaluations

- What method of doing the dots for "i" and "j" feel most comfortable and suit your preferred visual language?
- How are your t's and x's? You may wish to practice them until they feel comfortable and you don't have to think about them so much.
- How much does your quilted writing resemble your written writing?

Exercise: Echo Quilting

Echo quilting adds rich texture to your quilts because it allows you to emphasize certain designs or shapes. In echo quilting, you quilt an outline around a design and then *echo* around it repeatedly. Each time, you stitch another outline that is roughly ¼" (or whatever distance that you choose) outside the previous outline. Echo quilting looks great when used to quilt around appliqué designs and it can also be fantastic around a central quilted motif. The more echoes you add the more the central motif stands out from the quilting.

The trick to echo quilting is good visibility—to stitch around a design, you need to be able to see it. You also may need to stitch slower than usual. Use the edge of your darning foot to guide distance. At the same time, allow yourself to be a beginner. The consistent inconsistencies that happen will add an energy to the stitching that is distinctly yours.

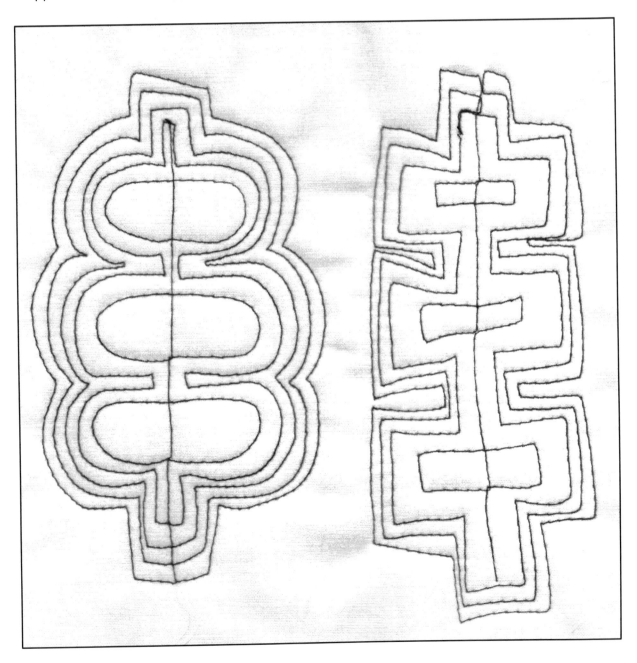

Wavy Lines…

Here, wavy lines are echoed. This makes a great background fill. You can choose how wavy you want the lines to be and how close together they are echoed. Allow your consistent inconsistencies to shine—this is your voice, your style—the very marks of your hand and heart.

Just quilt and quilt echoed lines and see how the gorgeous texture develops.

Organic Spiral Echoes...

This pattern began with three separate concentric circles, stitched from the inside out. Notice how the transition from concentric ring to the next creates a vertical line, which adds an interesting design element. Create three concentric circles and enlarge them until they just about touch. Then echo quilt around the three circles. You can use this same general stitching pattern around other combinations of shapes and motifs.

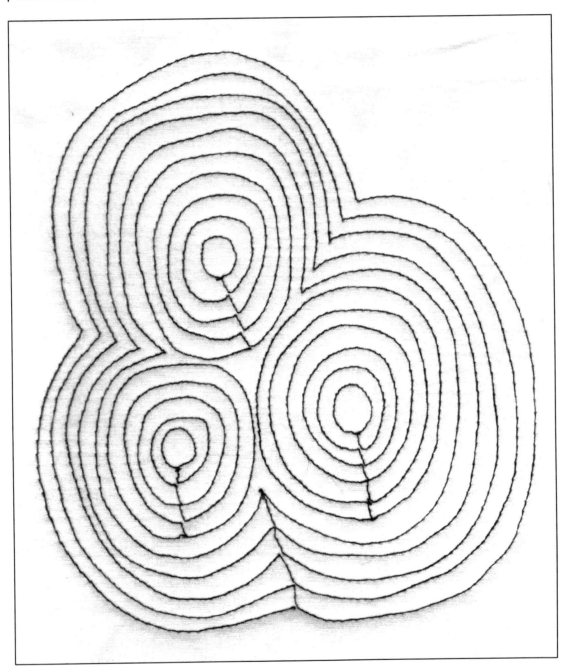

Echoes to Fill the Space...

You can use echoing lines to fill a background space. Here, a leaf motif is the central design element, and the echoing lines create an interesting chevron effect. Areas that are stitched less heavily, like the leaf shape, will come forward, and the heavily stitched echo quilting will cause the background to recede. This combination of textures adds visual interest to your quilt, and the less heavily quilted areas will become the focus.

Echoes to Bring Things Together

Here, begin with a flower center (circle), then stitch petals spiraling around. Add leaves and spiral around the entire design.

Gentle Evaluations

o   Do you have good visibility in your sewing machine setup for echo quilting?

Exercise: Patterns Based on Baptist Fans

Baptist Fan quilting is another all-over quilting design made of concentric traveling arcs. You can create smooth arcs or arcs that look like gears or even arcs that look like clouds or blossoms.

Smooth Baptist Fans...

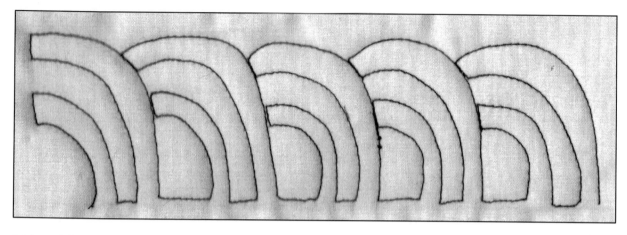

Industrial Gears...

Blooming Blossoms or Puffy Clouds...

There are a couple of tricks to stitching concentric traveling arcs. The first trick is understanding how the number of arcs determines on which side of the arc that you end.

- ○ Even numbers of passes means that you end on the same side of the arc from where you began (as shown in the two examples at left).
- ○ Odd numbers of passes means that you end on the opposite side of the arc from where you began (as shown in the two examples at right).

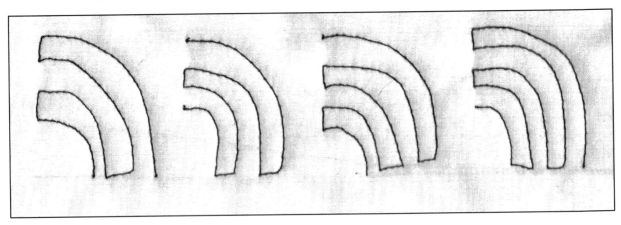

You can use this knowledge to your advantage as you begin to stitch overall Baptist Fan patterns.

The traditional way to build Baptist Fan patterns is to stitch them in rows. To stitch in rows, you want to use an **even** number of passes. Begin the row starting along the line you want to travel.

If you want the row to grow horizontally, then start the first arc on the bottom edge.

If you want the row to grow vertically, then start the first arc on the side edge.

Note in both examples that the arcs travel along the edges that have already been stitched. This hides the traveling.

Practice stitching smooth Baptist fan patterns in rows.

Organic Baptist Fan Background…

Another option for Baptist fan patterns is to build them in a more organic way, which fills the space without an obvious pattern of rows. In the example below, I started in the lower left corner. Notice how I alternated between odd and even numbers of passes to fill the space organically.

Blooming Blossoms or Puffy Clouds

Once you've learned the basics of building Baptist Fan patterns, you can modify them by adding different types of shapes. Here, puffy clouds or flower petals build a light and whimsical design.

Begin each art set with three smooth arcs for the flower center and then add two or three more echoing bumpy arcs to make the petals.

Industrial Gears

Here, the whimsical flowers become mechanical gears for a more industrial appearance. Begin each set of arcs with three smooth arcs for the gear center and then add two or three more echoing geared arcs.

This pattern can really challenge you because it combines curves and 90° angles. So it's a syncopated rhythm of smooth curves and then angled gears.

Peacock Feathers or Paisley Shapes

Here, concentric arcs become teardrops to create peacock feathers or paisley shapes. You can build them organically to create a dynamic background or alternate them along a center spine to create a feather shape.

Gentle Evaluations

- o Experiment with stitching in rows and then in all-over patterns. Does one method feel more comfortable?
- o What other ways can you alter the general Baptist Fan pattern to create your own design?

Exercise: Orange Peel Designs

The orange peel design is a traditional quilting design that can easily translate to free-motion quilting. It's an impressive pattern that is surprisingly easy and fun to stitch. You don't need to mark anything if you use eyeball estimation.

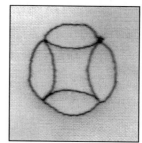

The orange peel is an interlocking pattern made of scalloped almond shapes. Each orange peel circle shares almonds with its neighbors.

To quilt the orange peel pattern, you alternate two rows until the pattern fills the desired space. And then you quilt a finishing row to complete the pattern. .

The first stitch pass sets up the top edges of the scalloped shape. This is stitched from left to right.

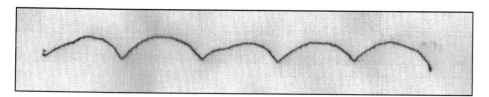

The second stitch pass creates the almonds for the top row and the vertical almonds. It is stitched from right to left. Notice that the leftmost almond remains unfinished—you will finish this at the end with the finishing row.

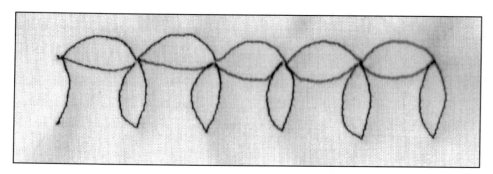

Repeat these two rows until you have filled the space as much as you want. Then end with the first row, as shown in the picture on the next page.

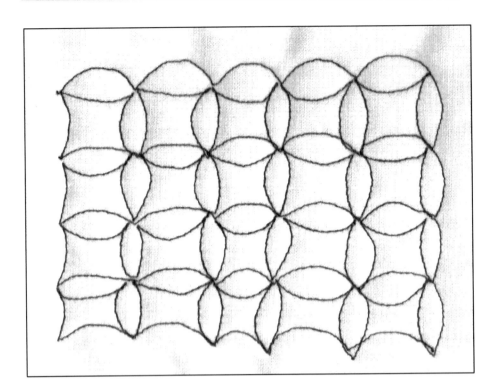

Stitch the finishing row from right to left, which completes the almonds of the bottom row, but does not add the vertical almonds. When you get to the end of the row, continue upwards to complete the almonds along the left side of the design.

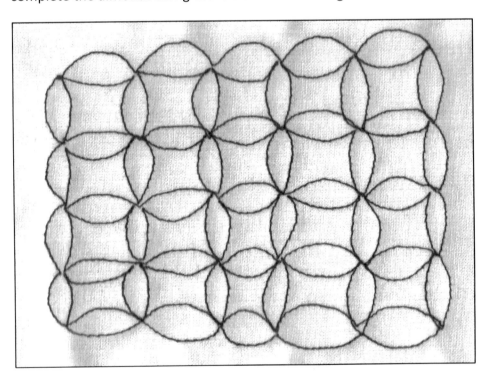

Discovering Your Visual Language

We all see the world in our own unique ways. Take ten people, give them each a camera, and send them to a scenic country location. Ask them to take photos of the things they see that inspire and move them. Their photos will reflect how their interests differ. Each will be captivated by different aspects of the location. Someone may capture the way the clouds roll over the horizon. Another may focus on the way the rustic barn creates a graphic composition of squares and planes. Someone else may be drawn to the cows munching contentedly on their hay. And another may spot tiny clusters of wildflowers along the fence posts.

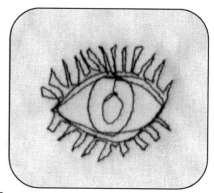

These differences reflect the many different ways that we see the world. Taking our lead from what inspires us is what will make our quilts uniquely ours. To begin to discover your visual language, you only need a few simple tools.

The simplest tools are those you carry around with you all the time: **your eyes, heart, and mind**. Look around you mindfully, both at art that you might encounter and at the everyday world. Ask yourself questions about what you see. "Why do I like this? Why don't I like that? And are there similarities among the things I like? Or among things I don't like?" Answering these questions with help you discover your own personal inspiration. Don't worry if your answers are vague and based more on how the piece makes you feel than an understanding of the principles of art. As you continue to look and learn, you'll be better able to verbalize exactly what it is that you like or don't like.

What inspires you visually? What knocks your socks off when you see it? This doesn't have to be limited to quilts or art. Maybe you love looking at foreign stamps or find old barns beautiful. What is it about the stamps that you love? Is it the color scheme, the exotic patterns, or how they evoke your love of travel? The reason you love old barns is idiosyncratic to you. Perhaps you love the texture of old wood and peeling paint. Or maybe it's the connection to the rural life that speaks to you. Or perhaps, like me, you see old barns as abstract compositions of color and shape.

Look at the world around you and think about what you see. Reflect on how it makes you feel. Look deeply with your eyes, and feel it with your heart. Find your deep inspiration in the wonders of our world.

A Note for Non-Doodlers

So you don't doodle? May I make one suggestion? Just start. Force yourself to develop a doodle habit. I use the word *force* intentionally because that may be what you have to do to begin. To doodlers, picking up a pen and making marks feels very comfortable. But to non-doodlers, making marks can feel very awkward. I should know, because I am a non-doodler who became an avid doodler.

How did I make that happen? By sitting down, picking up a pen, and making myself make marks. Even when I didn't know what to do, I made myself move pen on paper. I carried a notebook and pen with me and used those found moments while waiting for an appointment or sitting in a café to make marks. When I began carrying my notebook, I felt very self-conscious. But I persisted and doodled in it even when it felt forced and uncomfortable. Now it's much a part of who I am. And I feel lost when I forget to bring it.

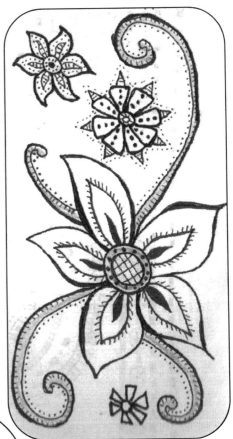

When you begin, don't worry about creating quilting designs. At this point, you just want to become comfortable holding the pen in your hand and making marks. Eventually, you will start to see patterns arise—shapes or patterns that you consistently doodle. You are becoming a doodler and can then begin to examine your doodles for shapes and lines that would make great quilting designs.

A Note for Doodlers

Do you doodle? Do you pick up a pen and doodle away while on the phone or at a meeting? If so, then those doodle patterns become great fodder for designing your own free-motion quilting designs. The marks you make while doodling are within you—you already have the muscle memory and the comfort of making art decisions with them. These designs are part of your visual language, which is why you feel comfortable when doodling them.

You can use this to your advantage. Examine your doodles for lines and shapes that can become quilting designs. Look for things that you can draw continuously—that is, shapes or lines that you doodle without lifting the pen from the page. Or take an existing doodle and think about how you can draw it in one continuous line. You may need to double-back in some areas, but that is perfectly fine—many continuous line quilting designs require that.

Let's say you doodle flowers like this, where each petal is a distinct shape that you draw separately.

To make it a continuous pattern you would start by drawing the flower center, then draw the petals circling around the center, connecting one to the next. Just eyeball the distance between them and make them fit. When you connect the last petal to the first, you can add the leaf. To add the second leaf you just need to travel around the outside edge of your petals and then add the second leaf. Or, to add the second leaf, you could travel back towards the flower center, circle around, and then come out between two petals. Either way works great.

Exercise: Stitching Radiating Motifs

Motifs that radiate around a center space look great standing alone. These often look like spokes on a wheel and include suns, flowers, and decorative motifs. There are ways to stitch them with a continuous line connecting one to the next, but I prefer them to stand alone. Stitching motifs individually does mean that you need to stop and start between each one, but that doesn't add too much extra time.

Spiral Sun…

- ❍ Begin in the center of the sun and spiral out as large as you want the sun center to be.
- ❍ Radiate the rays perpendicular to the place on the curve.
- ❍ Notice that there is a small gap at the base of each ray. This helps give the ray presence so it looks more like a ray and less like a leaf.

Other radiating designs...

Doodle and design your own radiating motifs. Use these examples for your inspiration.

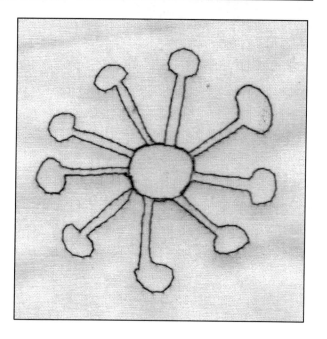

Exercise: Botanicals

Explore plants for inspiration. Doodle and design your own Botanical motifs.

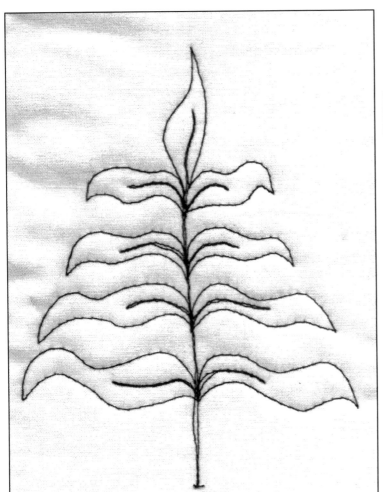

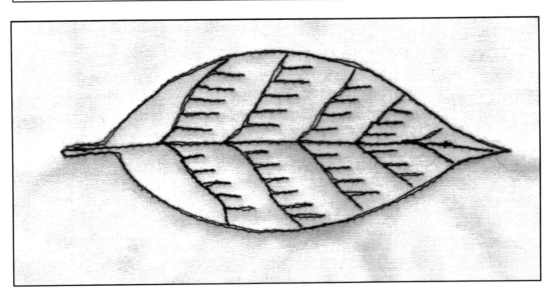

Exercise: Block Letters

This block letter pattern is just a fun one I devised while quilting the word RELAX as a reminder illustration earlier in this book.

Practice vs. Game Day; Or, Let's Talk about Performance Anxiety

At some point, you have practiced enough and it is time to quilt something for real. If you have ever played or coached sports or performed in plays or band or choruses, then you know that there is a qualitative difference between practice focus and intensity and game-day or performance focus and intensity. The same holds true for quilting.

When we practice on a muslin quilt sandwich, we feel free and perhaps even relaxed because we know that practice doesn't "count." When we go to quilt something "real," the way we feel may change. We can feel inspired and excited to use our skills on a real quilt or we might feel anxious and stifled because we are scared of messing it up. How we feel about quilting changes based on our attitude.

If you find yourself freezing up at the thought of quilting for "real," you can try a couple of things. Just as sports teams go through pre-season games before the season begins for "real" and performers have a dress rehearsal before performing for "real," you can practice for "real." Instead of choosing your hand-appliquéd modern Baltimore album as your first FMQ project, you can start by choosing a simpler quilt top.

Maybe you have a quilt top that has been languishing in the dark corner of a closet because it doesn't thrill you. Pull it out and use it for your quilting preseason. Or choose one of the simple quilt patterns at the back of this book to use as for "real" practice. You'll get a chance to practice on something that matters, but doesn't fill you with anxiety.

And know that any nervousness you feel is normal too. We choose our fabrics and piece with care, so we want to quilt well too. That is understandable. Just remember to allow yourself the freedom to be a learner, and make choices that provide you that freedom.

Exercise: How to Manage All That Bulk

Managing All That Bulk

Someone once described machine quilting as "wrestling with an alligator." Home sewing machines have a relatively small throat (the area between the needle and motor casing). When you consider the bulk of even a small throw quilt, you can imagine the difficulty of maneuvering that bulky material through a small throat hole. There are, however, some hints that will help you wrestle that gator.

If you can, set up your sewing table so that it is against a wall, which will keep the quilt from falling over the far edge of the table as you quilt. Set up an ironing board (at table height) or a card table to your left to help support the bulk of the quilt. Consider investing in a cabinet or large extension table so you have a larger surface to slide the quilt on.

Some machine quilters suggest rolling up the quilt for quilting. I find that to be more challenging; kind of like trying to maneuver a telephone pole under the machine. Instead, what I do is puddle or pool the quilt on my table, making sure that the weight of the quilt is supported by the table and not hanging over the edge of my table. Another thing to watch for is that the quilt edges stay visible. They like to slip under the bulk of the quilt and you can unwittingly sew several layers of the quilt together.

If your hands slip on the quilt, try quilting gloves. Quilting gloves, which have grippy fingers and palms, make it easier to handle the quilt. You can purchase these at your local quilt shop.

Remember to start quilting from the center and work your way out to the edges. A pin-basted quilt can be heavy and awkward to maneuver. I often begin using a walking foot to do machine-guided quilting in the ditch, which allows me to remove pins as I go. The machine-guided quilting holds the layers together nicely and allows me to free-motion quilt without having to stop and remove pins. It's also much lighter to quilt without the added weight of the pins. So you might want to consider where you place the safety pins so that you can stitch in the ditch.

Choosing Quilting Designs

There are so many different approaches to choosing quilting designs that I could write an entire book. Instead, I will offer you a couple of ideas to consideration and share with you the two techniques I use to audition quilting designs.

One is to consider the underlying structure of the quilt. Is it linear? Blocks? A one-patch? Curvilinear? Freeform? You can choose quilting designs that echo the underlying structure of the quilt. Or choose an overall design that serves as a counterpoint to the underlying structure. For example, a strictly linear quilt design can look very different when quilted with concentric circles than when quilted with an overall meandering pattern. The quilted circles serves as a interesting counterpoint to the linear horizontal nature of the quilt, whereas the overall meandering provides a blended appearance.

You can also use your fabric and block choices to inspire your design choices. If you used lots of botanical fabrics, you may want to use a leafy vine as the quilting pattern. If your quilt showcases lots of star blocks, you could quilt stars joined by meandering. If you used your collection of cat fabrics, try quilting little mice or paw prints.

I use two different methods to audition quilting designs depending on the scale of the area I am quilting. One is to place **clear vinyl on top of a quilt** and then mark the design on the vinyl. The other is to **print out a photograph of the quilt** and draw designs on the print out.

I use the **clear vinyl method** when I am auditioning designs for particular areas of smaller quilts. For example, one quilt (24" x 26") was a still life of a kitchen table, with a teapot, teacup and

saucer, spoon, and vase. I placed clear vinyl on the different elements of the quilt top, say the body of the tea pot, and used a washable marker to draw different quilting ideas on the vinyl. This allowed me to see exactly how the quilting designs I was considering would interact with the fabric and shape of the element.

It is **super important** to use masking tape to create a boundary around all the edges of the clear vinyl as shown in the picture at right. This keeps you from accidentally drawing the design off the edge of the vinyl and onto the quilt.

It is also **super important** to be careful when using markers of any kind around your quilt top. I use washable markers so that I can wash out any accidental marks that I make. But washing out is not always guaranteed, so be vigilant!

I use the **printed photograph method** when auditioning overall designs or how designs in certain areas interact with designs in other areas. I try to take a photograph of the quilt from as straight on as I can. (Software packages such as Photoshop allow you to straighten the photos as well.) Then I print several copies. I can draw potential quilting designs directly on the print-outs and use the ones I prefer.

Quilt Idea: Rag Quilt

If you are ready to begin using your free-motion quilting skills on a project, try a rag quilt. Rag quilts are the perfect avenue for learning.

Making rag quilts differs from making traditional quilts. Instead of piecing the quilt top, adding borders, basting, and then quilting, you quilt each block individually and only piece them together at the end. This means that you are only maneuvering a small quilt sandwich under the sewing machine, which allows you to focus on creating the quilting designs without having to wrestle with a larger quilt under the throat.

I always remind my students that rag quilts are meant to be used and loved, so any bobbles and blips from your learning just add to the cozy charm.

And, since you do not prewash the fabric before creating the rag quilt, when you wash and dry it the fabric shrinks a bit so your quilting creates a wonderful bumpy texture that is reminiscent of antique quilts. This adds to the comfy coziness and beautifully hides any glitches in the quilting.

The rag quilt described in this project measures 48" x 68" (before washing), but you can create your own version any size you want. The important thing to know is that you need to cut your batting squares at least 1" smaller than the fabric squares, which makes the ragged seam allowance. (You can choose to make the batting squares even smaller, say 10" fabric squares and 8" batting, which would create an even raggier appearance.) Just remember to quilt only through the fabric-covered batting—don't quilt in the extra fabric areas because that will keep the fabrics from ragging properly.

Supplies

- ½-yard cuts of 12 different fabrics (while flannels and homespuns are traditionally used in rag quilts, cottons and even batiks fray well)
- twin-size cotton batting
- rotary cutter, mat, and ruler
- cotton thread that coordinates or contrasts with your fabric—this will be your quilting thread
- basting spray, such as 505
- chalk wheel or other marking tool
- sharp scissors for snipping seams
- darning foot (for quilting the blocks)
- walking foot (for stitching the blocks together)

Cutting and Block Preparation

1) From each of your twelve fabrics, cut eight 9" squares, for a total of 96 squares.

2) From the batting, cut forty-eight 8" squares.

3) Make forty-eight quilt sandwiches by centering a batting square between two fabric squares. Use the same fabric for the top and bottom when making your quilt sandwiches. Secure the layers using basting spray.

IMPORTANT Quilting Guidelines

Always bring the bobbin thread to the top of your quilt sandwich before doing any stitching. By doing so, you avoid the jams that result when the bobbin thread gets pulled down by the feed dogs and the unsightly mess that happens when you sew over the bobbin thread.

To bring the bobbin thread to the top, place the quilt sandwich under your presser foot where you would like to begin stitching. Take one stitch by hand, using the flywheel. Make sure that you complete the stitch by raising the needle to its highest position. Tug on the top thread and the bobbin thread should rise to the top of your quilt sandwich. Hold both top and bottom threads out of the way.

Whenever you begin or end a line of stitching on your rag quilt, you need to secure the threads so your stitches don't come undone. The easiest way to do that is to set your straight stitch to a short length (.5 mm or 20 stitches per inch). Take 4-5 tiny stitches to secure your ends. Then quilt the block as desired. Don't forget to end your stitching with tiny stitches as well.

Make sure to quilt close to the edge of the batting on all sides—this keeps the batting from bunching up when washed. Do not quilt past the batting into the ½" space on the block edge.

Quilting the Blocks

Use a darning foot and drop your feed dogs to practice your free-motion quilting. You may wish to try a different type of quilting pattern for each fabric. For example, meander quilt all the red dotted squares. Feel free to explore your own designs. Remember, this is a quilt that is meant to be used and loved, so let that freedom inspire you!

Joining the Blocks

1) Layout your 48 blocks in a 6 blocks x 8 blocks pattern.

2) Using a ½" seam allowance, join 6 blocks together in a row. Sew the blocks with wrong-sides together so the wonderfully raggy seams appear on the right side. Sew 8 rows of 6 blocks.

3) Press all seams open.

4) Using a ½" seam allowance, join the 8 rows together. Place the rows wrong-sides together. Pin at intersections, if desired.

5) When the entire rag quilt is pieced together, stitch around the outside edge of the quilt, ½" in from edge.

Ragging the Quilt

1) Clip the seam allowances almost, but not quite, to the seam. Avoid clipping the seam because it can create a hole in the quilt top that lets batting escape when washing. Make clips ¼" to ½" apart. The closer your clips are, the raggier your quilt will be.

2) Wash your quilt. You may wish to do this at the laundromat to protect your washing machine and/or septic system.

3) After washing, shake quilt to remove loose threads.

4) Dry using medium heat for more shrinkage. While drying, empty the lint trap frequently to prevent overheating.

5) If needed, after drying, use your vacuum's brush attachment to clean up loose threads.

Enjoy Your Rag Quilt!

About KimberlyDavis

For over a decade, Kimberly Davis has inspired and guided women to discover their creative hearts through **Stitch Your Art Out**, the quilting and knitting shop that she co-owns just outside State College, Pennsylvania. She's passionate about sharing her deep love for the creative process with other women. She teaches class, leads workshops, and hosts retreats all with the intention to help women discover or deepen their journey on the creative path.

She lives outside State College, Pennsylvania with her husband and three cats, where she loves creating, painting, and spending time in nature.

Learn more about her quilting and knitting shop at www.stitchyourartout.com.

And learn more about her art and creative process at www.riverstonestudio.com.

Photo credits, Cynthia Spencer

- Author Portrait (page 114 and back cover)
- Presser Feet (page 11)
- Sketchbook (page 12)
- Hands and Sewing Machine (page 23)

Made in the USA
Middletown, DE
19 February 2015